ALLEN CARR'S

EASY WAY
TO
STOP SMOKING

US EDITION

This first US edition published for Allen Carr's Easyway
(International) Ltd. by:

Clarity Marketing
Allen Carr USA, 576 Fifth Ave, Suite #903, New York, NY 10036

This book is not intended to take the place of medical advice from
a trained medical professional.

Printed and bound in the USA

Library of Congress Control Number: 2011933692

ISBN: 978-0-6154-8215-6

Dedication

To all the smokers I have failed to cure personally,
I hope it will help them to get free.

To Damian O'Hara, in recognition of his fantastic
work in helping spread Allen Carr's Easyway
throughout the USA.

Also to Sid Sutton.

But most of all, to Joyce.

CONTENTS

FOREWORD TO
THE US EDITION

Allen Carr saved my life.

I was the smoker everyone said could never quit. I had my first cigarette as a nine-year-old, behind the proverbial bike shed, to try to impress one of my older brother's friends. That first cigarette was truly disgusting, but it didn't stop me from becoming a heavy smoker for twenty-six years. I rarely smoked less than a pack and a half a day, and if I was in an especially stressful situation at work or out drinking, I would literally chain-smoke.

Over the years, almost imperceptibly, smoking came to control my life: it controlled where I went, what I did, who I saw, who I avoided trying to see, where I ate, drank and worked. Of course, I didn't see it that way at all. In fact, like many smokers, I came to see the cigarette as my best friend, my 'me' time, my island of peace and tranquility in a crazy world, my ever-present companion.

At the same time, like all smokers, I knew it was killing me. For years I watched smoking decimate my family—grandparents, uncles and aunts. The tragedy was incredibly sad and stressful, and while it definitely made me want to quit, it also made me want to smoke more.

I tried to quit dozens of times. I was what we call a "serial quitter". But most of my attempts lasted just a couple of minutes before I had a "nic fit" and found myself rummaging around in the garbage, looking for my smokes. I promised my wife that when she got pregnant I would quit. I didn't. I told her when the baby was born I'd quit. The first thing I did after the birth was to light a big, fat cigar. In fact, things became so bad that I almost gave up trying to give up. I resigned myself to what was a truly depressing thought—being a smoker for the rest of my life.

Then in January 2001, I suffered a terrible bout of tonsillitis. Anyone who has experienced it will testify to the excruciating agony. I couldn't eat, talk, breathe or swallow, let alone smoke. For the first time in over twenty years, I went a whole day without smoking. To my astonishment, my head didn't explode, the earth continued its orbit around the sun and the universe did not disappear down a black hole.

I made the mistake of mentioning this to my wife who promptly suggested that I might think about going to an Allen Carr's Easyway seminar. She had quit back in 1992, just before we met, by reading the first edition of this book. Being the wonderful, thoughtful and caring person she is, she never tried to ram it down my throat, or threaten to leave me if I didn't quit. But she knew that one day I would be ready to quit and I will forever be in her debt for making that suggestion that I attend the seminar. I can only think that the pain meds slightly scrambled my thinking, and I agreed to go.

At the time (January is our busiest period, with all those New Year's resolutions!) there was a long waiting list to attend and so I was notified that I would be attending on February 21, 2001. Of course, by that time my tonsillitis was long gone, I was back smoking heavily and had no intention of quitting.

On the morning of the seminar, I told my wife that I was thinking of not going, but the look on her face told me otherwise (if you knew my wife you would know that when she gives you "the look," you don't mess with her). Eventually I agreed to attend, but I told her I was attending not to quit smoking, but to get our money back (all Allen Carr centers offer a money-back guarantee). "Whatever," she said, giving me the look once more.

At one o'clock that day I found myself sitting in Allen Carr's center in Raynes Park, near Wimbledon, just outside London along with seventeen other terrified smokers. I could barely see Cris, the facilitator, through the blue fog of smoke (in those days attendees were able to smoke throughout the session. Today, due to smoking by-laws, the sessions now feature regular smoke breaks).

Five minutes into the session I remember thinking "If I'm stuck in this room for the next five hours, I may as well listen to what these guys have to say." I listened to Cris talk about smoking, about quitting and about nicotine. There were no scare tactics, no pictures of diseased lungs and no guilt trips. Despite thinking that I already knew everything there was to know about smoking, many of the concepts he explained were completely new to me—I had just never really thought about smoking this way before. I found myself agreeing with everything he said. As the day wore on, I found my desire to smoke faded. By the time Cris instructed us to smoke our final cigarette, I could barely light it.

But I was dreading leaving the seminar because I knew that as soon as I got in my car to drive home, the terrible cravings would come—after all, I used to chain-smoke in my car. The cravings didn't come. I remember thinking that was odd, but not all that surprising because I had just spent five hours smoking heavily. After dinner, I thought—that's when they'll come. They didn't.

As I smoker, I used to light a cigarette as soon as I woke up, then stumble downstairs to spark up some coffee. I wasn't even human until at least my second coffee and my third cigarette. The following morning I didn't even think about smoking. Lighting a cigarette literally did not occur to me. I was stunned.

Smoking had gone from being the center of my life to being a total irrelevance in just five hours. I couldn't believe it, and neither could my family, my friends and colleagues. The only person who wasn't surprised was my wife, who just shrugged her shoulders and said: "See, it's easy!"

The changes in my life came thick and fast. I felt truly free and truly happy for the first time in years. I had more energy. I lost weight. I was able to concentrate longer and harder. Instead of looking for excuses to be away from my family so I could smoke, I felt re-engaged with them. It was fantastic. I'm ashamed to admit it now but stopping smoking enabled me to be a better husband and a much, much better father. I was shocked to notice the extent to which smoking had controlled my life and relationships.

Three months after attending, I wrote to Allen to thank him for helping me escape and to offer my help in spreading the word. In September 2001, I was privileged to be chosen to represent Allen Carr's Easyway in North America.

From late in 2001, Allen became a close friend and mentor to me. He was an amazing man—generous, intelligent and funny but also down-to-earth, passionate and approachable.

He was fascinated by the US. He traveled to Las Vegas every year for over twenty years to indulge his passion for poker. He was a great student of the American culture and psyche. He always felt that the Easyway method—with its positive, empowering approach to quitting—would especially resonate with Americans. And he was right—Americans took to the Easyway method like ducks to water.

Over the years, Allen and I spent endless hours discussing Easyway in the US and how to further improve its effectiveness by adapting and refining it for the American market. In particular, we discussed the differences between American and European smokers and their responses to the method. This brand new US edition of *Allen Carr's Easyway to Stop Smoking* benefits by incorporating not only the core of Allen's unique Easyway method that has worked wonderfully for so many smokers over the past twenty-five years, but also ten years of learning, experience and feedback we have had since starting to work with smokers in North America in 2001.

We thank the thousands of Americans who have successfully used Allen Carr's Easyway for their invaluable feedback in putting this US edition together, and for their continued support in spreading the Easyway message.

On a personal level, I would like to dedicate this new US edition of *Easyway* to the two men who have had the biggest influence on my life: my mentor, the incomparable Allen Carr, and my hero and best friend—my late father Jack O'Hara. The world is a poorer place now that you're gone, but it's inestimably richer for your having lived.

Damian O'Hara
Allen Carr's Easyway North America

PREFACE

Just suppose there were a magic method of stopping smoking which enables any smoker, including you, to quit:

- IMMEDIATELY
- PERMANENTLY
- WITHOUT NEEDING WILLPOWER
- WITHOUT SUFFERING WITHDRAWAL SYMPTOMS
- WITHOUT PUTTING ON WEIGHT
- WITHOUT SHOCK TACTICS, PILLS, PATCHES OR OTHER GIMMICKS

Let's further suppose that:

- THERE IS NO INITIAL PERIOD OF FEELING DEPRIVED OR MISERABLE
- YOU IMMEDIATELY ENJOY SOCIAL OCCASIONS MORE

- YOU FEEL MORE CONFIDENT AND BETTER EQUIPPED TO HANDLE STRESS
- YOU ARE BETTER ABLE TO CONCENTRATE
- YOU DON'T HAVE TO SPEND THE REST OF YOUR LIFE HAVING TO RESIST THE OCCA-SIONAL TEMPTATION TO LIGHT A CIGARETTE

And

- YOU NOT ONLY FIND IT EASY TO QUIT, BUT CAN ACTUALLY ENJOY THE PROCESS FROM THE MOMENT YOU EXTINGUISH THE LAST CIGARETTE

If there were such a magical method, would you use it?

Chances are you would. But of course you don't believe in magic. Neither do I. Nevertheless the method I describe above does exist. I call it EASYWAY. In fact it isn't magic, it just seems that way. It certainly seemed that way to me when I first discovered it and I know that many of the millions of ex-smokers who have successfully quit with the help of EASYWAY also view it in that light.

No doubt you find my claims difficult to believe. Don't worry; I would regard you as somewhat naive if you just accepted them without proof. On the other hand, do not make the mistake of dismissing them out of hand because they sound far-fetched. In all probability you are only reading this book because of the recommendation of an ex-smoker who attended an Allen Carr's EASYWAY seminar, read this book or stopped using another Allen Carr product. It doesn't matter whether you received the recommendation directly or via someone who loves you and is desperately worried that unless you quit, you won't be there to go on loving.

How does EASYWAY work? That is not easy to describe briefly. Smokers arrive at our seminars in differing states of panic, convinced that they won't succeed and believing that even if by some miracle they do manage to quit, they will first have to endure a long period of abject misery, that social occasions will never quite be so enjoyable, that they will be less able to concentrate and cope with stress and that, although they may never smoke again, they will never be completely free and that for the rest of their lives they will have occasional yearnings to smoke a cigarette and will have to resist temptation.

The majority of those smokers leave the seminar a few hours later already happy non-smokers. How do we achieve that incredible transformation? Most smokers would expect us to achieve that objective by telling them of the terrible health risks they run, that smoking is a filthy, disgusting habit that costs them a fortune, and that they are stupid not to quit. No. We do not patronize them by telling them what they already know. These are the problems of being a smoker. They are not the problems of quitting. Smokers do not smoke for the reasons that they *shouldn't* smoke. In order to quit it is necessary to remove the reasons they *do* smoke. EASYWAY addresses these problems. It removes the desire to smoke. Once the desire to smoke has been removed, it doesn't take any willpower to quit.

The EASYWAY method exists in the form of seminars, books, DVDs, audiotapes, CD-ROMs, video games and webcasts. In each case the method is the same, they are merely different ways to communicate it. Which vehicle should you choose? It's a question of personal choice. Some people prefer reading books, others prefer watching DVDs or webcasts. The seminars enjoy such a high success rate that we are able to give a money-back guarantee. The fee varies according to location and if you are one of the 20% who requires more than one visit, you can attend any number of follow-ups without further charge.

We never give up on any smoker. And if you fail to stop smoking once the program is completed, your fee will be refunded in full. Fewer than 5% of attendees at our US seminars ask for a refund.

Do not let any of the above detract from the value of this book. It is a complete course in itself and millions of readers have quit easily simply by reading it. If you are in doubt, why not telephone your nearest Allen Carr's Easyway center for further guidance. A list of centers appears at the back of the book.

WARNING

Perhaps you are somewhat apprehensive about reading this book. Perhaps, like the majority of smokers, the mere thought of quitting fills you with panic and although you have every intention of stopping one day, it is not today.

If you are expecting me to inform you of the terrible health risks that smokers run, that smokers waste a fortune, that it's a filthy, disgusting habit and that you are a weak-willed jellyfish, then I must disappoint you. Those tactics never helped me to quit and if they were going to help you, you would already have quit.

My method, which I will refer to as EASYWAY, doesn't work that way. Some of the things I am about to say, you might find difficult to believe. However, by the time you've finished this book, you'll not only believe them, but wonder how you could ever have been brainwashed to believe otherwise.

There is a common misapprehension that we choose to smoke. Smokers no more choose to smoke than drinkers choose to become alcoholics, or heroin users choose to become junkies. It is true that we choose to light those first experimental cigarettes. I occasionally choose to go to the cinema, but I certainly wouldn't choose to spend the rest of my life there.

Think about that for a moment. Did you ever make the positive decision that you wouldn't be able to enjoy a meal or a social occasion without smoking, or that you wouldn't be able to concentrate or handle stress without a cigarette? At what stage did you decide that you needed cigarettes, not just for social occasions, but that you needed to have them permanently with you? At what point did you feel even panic-stricken, without them? What was the date you decided that you would be a smoker for the rest of your life, puffing away all day, every day, never being able to stop? The average American smoker smoked their first cigarette as a thirteen-year-old. Are we really saying that at thirteen we were deciding that we would be smokers until our dying day?

Of course not. Like every other smoker, we fell into a trap. The nicotine trap is the most subtle, sinister trap that man and nature have combined to devise. There is not a sane parent on this planet—smoker or non-smoker—that likes the thought of their children smoking. Surely this is because deep down, all smokers wish they had never started. It's not surprising really. No one needed cigarettes to enjoy meals or cope with stress before they got hooked.

At the same time all smokers want to quit, all smokers also want to keep smoking. After all, no one forces us to smoke—it is only smokers themselves who decide to light up.

If there were a magic button that smokers could press to wake up the following morning as if they had never lit that first cigarette, the only smokers left would be the youngsters who are still at the experimental stage, playing with fire, convinced they could never get hooked. Didn't we all start that way?

The truth is that the only thing that keeps us smoking, the only thing that prevents us from breaking free is FEAR!

We fear that as non-smokers, we will have to struggle through the rest of our lives feeling deprived and miserable; fear that we will need endless supplies of willpower to conquer the terrible cravings; fear that a meal or a social occasion will never be quite as enjoyable without a cigarette; fear that we'll never be able to concentrate, handle stress or be as confident without our little crutch; fear that our personality and character will change; but most of all, we fear that we will never be completely free, and that we will spend the rest of our lives wanting to smoke but not being allowed to.

If, as I did, you have already tried all the "conventional" ways to quit you will not only be dominated by those fears I describe, but also convinced you can never get free.

If you are apprehensive, panic-stricken or feel that the time is not right for you to stop, then you are being affected by the fear. As I will show throughout this book, that fear is not relieved by cigarettes but created by them. Non-smokers don't have any of these fears.

You didn't decide to fall into the nicotine trap. Like all traps, it is designed to ensure that you remain in it. Ask yourself, when you lit those first experimental cigarettes, did you think you would remain a smoker as long as you have? So when are you going to quit? Tomorrow? The next Great American Smokeout? New Year's Eve? Next year? Stop kidding yourself! The trap is designed to hold you for life. Why else do you think all those other smokers didn't quit before it killed them?

This book was first published in 1985. It has sold over 11,000,000 copies and been a bestseller every year since then. In putting together this brand new US edition, we are using over twenty-five years of feedback from both our seminars and previous editions. As you will soon be reading, that feedback has revealed information that has exceeded my wildest dreams regarding the effectiveness of EASYWAY. It has also revealed two aspects of the method that have caused me concern. The second I will cover in just a moment. The first arose out of the many letters I have received from readers. I give three typical examples:

"I didn't believe the claims you made and I apologize for doubting you. It was just as easy and enjoyable as you said it would be. I've given copies of your book to all my smoking friends and relatives, but I can't understand why they don't read it."

"I was given your book eight years ago by an ex-smoking friend. I've just got around to reading it and can't tell you how great it is to be free. My only regret is that I wasted eight years."

"I've just finished reading EASYWAY. I know it has only been four days, but I feel so great, I know I'll never need to smoke again. I first started to read your book five years ago, got halfway through and panicked. I knew that if I went on reading I would have to stop. Wasn't I silly?"

That particular young lady wasn't silly. I referred earlier to a magic button. Allen Carr's EASYWAY works just like that magic button. Let me make it quite clear, EASYWAY isn't magic, but for me and the millions of former smokers who have found it easy and enjoyable to quit, it seems like magic!

This is the warning. We have a chicken and egg situation. Every smoker wants to quit and every smoker can find it easy and enjoyable to do so. It's only fear that prevents smokers from trying to quit. The greatest benefit of quitting is to be rid of that fear. But you won't be free from it until you have completed the book. On the contrary, like the lady in the third example, that fear might even increase as you are reading and this might prevent you from finishing it.

You didn't decide to fall into this trap. When you were a youngster, just starting out as a smoker, you didn't even know the trap existed. You need to be very clear in your mind that you won't escape from it unless you make a positive decision to do so. You might already be straining at the leash to quit. On the other hand you may be apprehensive. Either way YOU HAVE ABSOLUTELY NOTHING TO LOSE!

If at the end of the book you decide that you want to continue smoking, there is nothing to prevent you from doing so. You don't even have to cut down or stop smoking while you're reading the book and remember: there is no shock treatment. Do you really think that the health warnings on cigarette packs scare smokers into quitting? If they do, why are one in five American adults still smoking?

On the contrary, I have nothing but good news for you. Can you imagine how Nelson Mandela must have felt when he was finally released from prison? That's how I felt when I escaped from the nicotine trap. That's how the millions of ex-smokers who have used my method feel. By the end of the book: THAT'S HOW YOU WILL FEEL! GO FOR IT!

INTRODUCTION

"I'm going to cure the world of smoking."

I was talking to my wife. She thought I'd finally flipped. Understandable if you consider that she had watched me fail to quit on countless previous occasions. The most recent had been two years previously. I'd actually survived six months of sheer hell before I finally caved in and lit a cigarette. I'm not ashamed to admit that I cried like a baby. I was crying because I knew that I was condemned to be a smoker for the rest of my life. I had put so much effort into that attempt and suffered so much misery that I knew I would never have the strength to go through that ordeal again. I'm not a violent man, but if some patronizing non-smoker had been stupid enough to suggest to me that all smokers can find it easy to quit, immediately and permanently, I would not have been responsible for my actions. However, I'm convinced that any jury in the world, comprised only of smokers, would have pardoned me on the grounds of justifiable homicide.

Perhaps you too find it impossible to believe that it can be easy to quit. If so, I beg you not to toss this book into the nearest trash can. Please trust me. I assure you it's true that any smoker—even you—can find it easy to quit.

Anyway, there I was two years later, having just put out what I knew would be my final cigarette, not only telling my wife that I was already a non-smoker, but that I was going to cure the rest of the world too. I must admit that at the time I found her skepticism somewhat irritating. However, in no way did it diminish my feeling of exaltation. I suppose that my exhilaration in knowing that I was already a happy non-smoker distorted my perspective somewhat. With the benefit of hindsight, I can sympathize with her attitude. I now understand why Joyce and my close friends and relatives thought I was a candidate for the funny farm.

As I look back on my life, it almost seems that my whole existence has been a preparation for solving the smoking problem. Even those hateful years of training and practicing as a chartered accountant were invaluable in helping me to unravel the mysteries of the smoking trap.

Abraham Lincoln once said that you can't fool all the people all the time, but that's exactly what I believe the tobacco companies have been successfully doing for decades. I also believe that I was the first person to really understand the smoking trap. Please don't mistake this statement for arrogance. I wish I could claim that my superior intellect led me to this understanding, but actually it was merely the circumstances of my own life.

The momentous day was July 15, 1983. I didn't escape from Alcatraz, but it felt like it. Even today, over twenty years later, I can still remember the feelings of relief, happiness and excitement when I stubbed out that final butt. I realized immediately that I had discovered something that every smoker secretly dreamed of: an easy way to stop smoking.

After testing out the method on smoking friends and relatives, I gave up accountancy and became a full-time counselor, running seminars to help other smokers to get free.

I wrote the first edition of this book in 1985. One of my failures, the man described in Chapter 25, was the inspiration.

He visited me twice, and we were both reduced to tears on each occasion. He was so agitated that I couldn't get him to relax enough to listen to what I was saying. I hoped that if I wrote it all down, he could read it in his own good time, as many times as he wanted, and this would help him absorb the message.

I was in no doubt that EASYWAY would work just as effectively for other smokers as it had for me. However, when I contemplated putting the method into book form, I was apprehensive. I did my own market research. The comments were not very encouraging:

> "How can a book help me to quit? What I need is willpower!"
>
> "How can a book help me cope with the terrible withdrawal pangs?"

In addition to these pessimistic comments, I also had my own doubts. During a seminar if it became obvious that a client had misunderstood an important point, I was able to correct the situation. But how would a book be able to do that? When I was studying to be an accountant and didn't understand or agree with a certain point in a book, I remember the frustration because I couldn't ask a book to explain. I was also well aware that many people were no longer accustomed to reading.

Added to all these factors, I had one doubt that overrode the rest. I wasn't a writer and was very conscious of my limitations in this respect. I was confident that I could sit down face to face with any smoker and convince them how easy and enjoyable the process of quitting can be, but could I translate that ability into the written word? Thankfully I needn't have worried. In the twenty-six years since EASYWAY first appeared on the shelves, we have received tens of thousands of letters and emails from grateful readers containing comments such as:

"It's the greatest book ever written."

"You are my guru."

"You are a genius."

"You should be knighted."

"You should be Prime Minister."

"You are a saint."

It is wonderful and humbling to receive letters such as these, and I hope that I have not allowed such comments to go to my head. I'm fully aware that those comments were made not to compliment me on my literary skills, but in spite of my lack of them. They were made because whether your preference is to read a book, watch an online webcast or to attend a seminar: ALLEN CARR'S EASYWAY METHOD WORKS!

Not only do we now have a network of over 150 seminar centers, including locations across the US, but this book has now been translated into more than forty languages. As I write, it is the number one non-fiction bestseller in Russia and it has also topped bestseller lists in Holland, Germany, France, Norway, Italy, Spain and the UK. It is rarely out of the top 50 bestsellers on Amazon's European websites, and it is one of their most reviewed books, receiving over 1,100 five-star ratings—the highest available. My Norwegian publisher tells me that when the wonderful *Harry Potter and the Order of the Phoenix* was launched, it did not dislodge EASYWAY from the number one spot!

After approximately a year of running stop smoking seminars, I thought I had learned everything there was to know about helping smokers to quit. Amazingly, I still learn something new practically every day. This fact caused me some concern when I was asked to review the original edition and write this brand new US one. I feared that I would have to amend or retract practically everything I had written.

Again, I needn't have worried. The basic principles of EASYWAY are as sound today as when I first committed them to paper in 1985. The beautiful truth is:

IT IS EASY TO STOP

This is a fact. My only challenge is to convince smokers that it's true.

At the seminars we try to achieve perfection. Every single failure hurts us deeply because we know that every smoker can find it easy to quit. When smokers fail, they tend to blame themselves but we regard the failure as ours—we fail to convince those smokers just how easy and enjoyable it is to quit and to stay quit. This is why we offer a money-back guarantee to all our seminar attendees. While initially this money-back concept nearly gave my bank manager a heart attack, over the past twenty-five years his fear has proved to be unfounded as fewer than 5% of attendees make a claim for a refund.

When I started to conduct seminars to help smokers, I originally believed that my biggest enemy would be the tobacco industry. While it is true that they have been less than friendly, amazingly my main obstacles have in fact been the very institutions that I thought would be my greatest allies: the media, the government and the tobacco control establishment.

I'm a fan of old movies and I recently watched the marvelous *Sister Kenny*. It's a somewhat obscure film from the 1940s starring Rosalind Russell. It tells the astonishing (and true) story of Sister Elizabeth Kenny, an Australian nurse who worked with children suffering from infantile paralysis or polio. During the first half of the twentieth century until the discovery of a vaccine in 1954, the word "polio" engendered the same fear as the word "cancer" does today. The effect of polio was not only to paralyze the legs and arms but also to distort them. The established medical treatment of the time was to put the limbs in irons in an attempt to prevent the distortion. The result was paralysis for life.

Sister Kenny rightly believed that the irons actually prevented recovery and demonstrated a thousand times over at her clinic that the muscles could be retrained to enable children to once again walk. However, Sister Kenny wasn't a doctor; she was merely a nurse. How dare she dabble in an area that was confined to qualified doctors? It didn't seem to matter that Sister Kenny had found a solution to the problem and had proved her solution to be effective. The children treated by Sister Kenny knew she was right; so did their parents. Yet the Australian medical establishment not only refused to adopt her methods but also banned her from practicing. In 1940, after thirty years of rejection, Sister Kenny moved to the US where she was eventually viewed as a miracle worker. In 1952 she was voted America's Most Admired Woman.

I first saw that film years before I discovered EASYWAY. It is a wonderful and entertaining story, but surely Hollywood had used a large slice of artistic license for dramatic effect? Sister Kenny couldn't possibly have discovered something that the medical establishment had failed to see for themselves. Surely the medical profession weren't the dinosaurs they were being portrayed as? How could it possibly have taken these intelligent, devoted men and women of science twenty years to accept the facts that were staring them in the face?

They say that fact is stranger than fiction. I apologize to the makers of *Sister Kenny* for accusing them of using artistic license. I now know first-hand the difficulties she faced. Like Sister Kenny, I'm just a lone individual without the support of the big pharmaceutical companies or the major tobacco control charities such as the American Cancer Society, the Lung Association or the Heart and Stroke Foundation. Like her, I'm only famous because my approach works. Like her, the medical establishment has ignored the experience of millions of real people who have successfully quit using my simple, drug-free approach. Like Sister Kenny, I naively thought that once the establishment had seen the efficacy of my approach, they would not hesitate to adopt it. I could not have been more wrong.

You might draw the conclusion that I am no respecter of the medical profession. Nothing could be further from the truth. One of my sons is a doctor and I know of no finer profession. Indeed we receive more referrals to our centers from the medical profession than any other source, and surprisingly, more of our clients come from the medical profession than from any other.

In the early years, I was regarded by the medical profession as being a combination of charlatan and quack. However, in August 1997, I had the great honor to be invited to address the 10th World Conference on Tobacco or Health, hosted by the World Health Organization, in Beijing. I believe I am the first person with no medical qualifications to receive such an honor. The invitation itself was a measure of the progress we have made in establishing EASYWAY in the mainstream of stop smoking methods. However, I was disappointed to find that my lecture fell on deaf ears. The attendees (mainly public health policymakers and tobacco researchers) seemed able only to think in terms of drug-based approaches to quitting (e.g., treating nicotine addiction by prescribing nicotine). This was fortunate and convenient, as the conference itself was sponsored by the manufacturers of nicotine replacement products.

It occurred to me at that conference that almost none of the people in the field of trying to help smokers to quit had ever been smokers themselves. They may have known the molecular structure of nicotine and the impact of continuous exposure to the tars contained in tobacco on the human body, but none of them really understood smokers and smoking. As a result, they knew absolutely nothing about the reality of quitting.

As a consequence of this enormous gap in their knowledge, the medical establishment's strategy was (and is to this day) to tell smokers what they already know: that they shouldn't smoke because it is disgusting, anti-social, dangerous and expensive. Let's face it, if this strategy worked, there wouldn't be any smokers. Smokers don't smoke for the reasons they shouldn't smoke—every smoker knows that already and if it were going to make them quit, it would have done so years ago.

Even today, the medical profession seems adamant that nicotine replacement products or anti-depressants need to be used when smokers are trying to stop. While we are told that such treatments "can double your chances" of quitting, the truth is that when all is said and done, such treatments have an 85–95% failure rate (depending on which research you read). Why doctors continue to prescribe treatments with such poor levels of success eludes me entirely, particularly when there is a fast, cheap alternative which has been proved effective many thousands of times over many years.

As I write this, the health authorities have just announced the launch of yet another media campaign aimed at discouraging children from starting to smoke by the use of frightening visual images. I recently appeared on TV along with a doctor representing Action on Smoking & Health (ASH), who had never smoked a day in her life and had never cured a single smoker. She categorically informed viewers that this campaign would discourage thousands of children from smoking and thereby save hundreds, or maybe thousands of lives. Sadly, the statistics don't give cause for such optimism. Studies from around the world show that levels of smoking amongst teenagers, particularly teenage girls, have never been higher.

I mention this because it demonstrates the profound lack of understanding that much of the health establishment has of smoking and smokers. So long as teenagers perceive smoking as cool, anti-establishment and a badge of independence and adulthood, they will experiment, irrespective of what the health establishment tells them about the long-term dangers. They know that one cigarette won't kill them, and believe they could never get hooked on something that tastes so disgusting. Isn't that how we all started?

It staggers me that the medical establishment hasn't yet figured out what every parent on the planet knows—that the best way to guarantee that our teenagers start smoking is to tell them not to.

In the original edition of this book I wrote:

"There is a wind of change in society. A snowball has started that I hope this book will help turn into an avalanche."

Twenty-five years and over 11,000,000 copies later, I think the snowball has grown into the size of a bowling ball, but it is still only a drop in the ocean. While the tobacco-control establishment pats itself on the back over their latest "victory," every year an estimated five million smokers will die as a direct result of their addiction and they will be replaced by over ten million new teenage smokers. This doesn't look, smell or sound like "victory" to me.

I'm immensely grateful to the millions of ex-smokers who have attended our seminars, read my books, watched the webcast and have recommended EASYWAY to their friends, relatives and colleagues and I dearly hope that they continue to do so.

It is this word of mouth that will turn the bowling ball into an avalanche. While the medical profession continues to prescribe the latest pill or potion (many of them actually containing the drug you are trying to kick), more and more smokers will turn to the common sense, painless solution offered by EASYWAY.

The truth is, as we have demonstrated countless thousands of times over the years, that it can be easy and enjoyable to stop smoking. Do you have a feeling of doom and gloom? Forget it. I've been lucky to achieve some wonderful things in my life. By far the greatest was to escape from the slavery of nicotine addiction. I escaped over twenty-five years ago and still can't get over the joy of being free. There is no need to feel miserable. There is nothing bad happening. On the contrary, you are about to achieve what every smoker on the planet would love to achieve: TO BE FREE!

CHAPTER 1

THE WORST
NICOTINE ADDICT
I EVER MET

Perhaps I should begin by describing my credentials for writing this book. No, I am not a doctor or a psychologist; my qualifications are far more relevant. I spent thirty-three years of my life as a hardcore smoker. In the later years I smoked a hundred a day on a bad day, and never less than sixty.

During my life I had made dozens of attempts to stop. I once stopped for six miserable months. I hated every minute of it, still standing near smokers trying to get a whiff of the tobacco.

With most smokers, it's a case of "I'll stop before something happens to me." The "something" was already happening to me. I already had reached the stage where I knew cigarettes were killing me. I had a permanent headache, which I thought was

1

normal, from the pressure of the constant coughing. I could feel the continuous throbbing of the vein that runs vertically down the center of my forehead, and I honestly believed that at any moment there would be an explosion in my head and I would die from a brain hemorrhage. It bothered me and it scared me, but it still didn't stop me from lighting the next one.

I had reached the stage where I gave up even trying to stop. It wasn't even that I enjoyed smoking. At some stage in their lives most smokers suffer from the illusion that they enjoy some cigarettes, but I didn't. I always detested the taste and smell, but I thought that a cigarette helped me to relax. It gave me courage and confidence, and I was always miserable when I tried to stop, never being able to visualize an enjoyable life without smoking.

During those awful years as a smoker I thought that my life depended on cigarettes and I was prepared to die rather than be without them. Today, over twenty-five years after I finally broke free from the slavery of smoking, people still ask me whether I ever have the odd pang. I truthfully answer: "Never, never, never"—just the reverse. I've had a marvelous life. If I had died through smoking I couldn't have complained. I have been a very lucky man, but the most marvelous thing that has ever happened to me is being freed from that nightmare, the slavery of having to go through life systematically destroying my own body and paying through the nose for the privilege.

Let me make it quite clear from the beginning: I am not a mystical figure. I do not believe in magic or fairies. I have a scientific, rational brain, and for quite a while after I quit, I couldn't understand why I found it to be so easy. It seemed like magic, but it couldn't have been. I started to read books on smoking, hypnosis and psychology. Nothing I read seemed to adequately explain what had happened. Why had it been so ridiculously easy to stop, whereas previously it had been week after agonizing week of torture and dark depression?

It took me a long time to work it all out, basically because I was going about it back to front. I was trying to work out why it was so easy to stop, whereas the real question ought to be: "Why should quitting be difficult?" Smokers talk about the terrible physical withdrawal pangs, but when I looked back and tried to remember those awful pangs, they didn't exist for me. There was no physical pain. It was all in the mind.

My full-time job for the last twenty-five years has been to help other people to stop smoking. I'm very, very successful. Every year 30,000–50,000 smokers attend our seminars. I have personally helped to cure many tens of thousands of smokers. Let me emphasize from the start: there is no such thing as a "confirmed" smoker. I have yet to meet anybody who was as badly hooked (or, rather, *thought* he was as badly hooked) as myself. Anybody can not only stop smoking but also find it easy. That is a fact. We prove this day-in, day-out at our seminar centers, which routinely help the hardest of hardcore smokers escape from the smoking trap easily and permanently. It is basically fear that keeps us smoking: the fear that life will never be quite as enjoyable without cigarettes and the fear of feeling deprived. In fact, nothing could be further from the truth. Not only is life just as enjoyable without them but it is infinitely more so. Incredibly, better health and a vastly improved financial position are the least of those gains.

All smokers can find it easy to stop smoking—even you! All you have to do is read the rest of the book with an open mind. The more you understand, the easier you will find it. Even if you do not understand every word, provided you follow the instructions you will find it easy. Most important of all, you will not go through life moping for cigarettes or feeling deprived. The only mystery will be why you didn't stop years ago.

At this point, let me issue a warning. There are only two reasons for failure with my method:

1. **Failure to Carry Out Instructions.** Some people find it annoying that I am so dogmatic about certain recommendations. For example, I will tell you not to try cutting

down or using substitutes, especially substitutes that contain nicotine (e.g., e-cigarettes, nicotine gum, patches, etc.). The reason I am so dogmatic is because I know my subject. I do not deny that many people have successfully stopped using such tools, but they have succeeded in spite of, not because of them. There are people who can make love standing on a hammock, but it is not the easiest or the most enjoyable way. Everything I tell you has a purpose: to ensure your success by making it easy and enjoyable to stop.

2. **Failure to Understand.** Please don't take anything for granted. Question not only what I tell you but also your own preconceptions and attitudes and what society has led you to believe about smoking and quitting. For example, if you think smoking is "just a habit," ask yourselves why other habits, some of them extremely enjoyable ones, are easy to break, yet a habit that tastes awful, costs us a fortune and kills us is so difficult. If you think you enjoy smoking, ask yourself why you absolutely *have* to smoke that cigarette, but can take or leave other things in life, which are infinitely more enjoyable.

CHAPTER 2

THE EASYWAY

The aim of this book is to get you into the frame of mind whereby instead of starting out on your smoke-free life with a feeling of doom, gloom, misery and depression, you can start right away with a feeling of elation, as if you have been cured of a terrible, life-threatening disease.

Smokers thinking about quitting are often intimidated by what they perceive to be the scale of the task they face. They feel as if they are attempting to scale Mount Everest single-handed. They believe that they will need to suffer terrible physical withdrawal pangs, that they are giving up their best friend and that they will, in all likelihood, fail anyway. Who could think of a worse frame of mind with which to take on this, or any other project? The smoker has already programmed him or herself to fail. But if you are able to replace those negative thoughts and feelings with an attitude of excitement and anticipation, then the task is made far easier. In fact, with the right frame of mind, it is not only easy, but also incredibly enjoyable to stop smoking. From then on, the further you go through life the more you will look at cigarettes and wonder how you had ever believed you needed to smoke. You will look at smokers with pity as opposed to envy.

Provided that you are not already a non-smoker or an ex-smoker, it is essential to keep smoking until you have finished the book completely. This may appear to be something of a contradiction. Later I shall be explaining that cigarettes do absolutely nothing for you at all. In fact, one of the many puzzles about smoking is that when we are smoking a cigarette, we look at it and wonder what on earth we are doing: it is only when we can't smoke that the cigarette becomes precious or desirable.

However, let us accept that, whether you like it or not, you believe you need to smoke and that you can't relax or concentrate properly unless you are smoking. So do not attempt to stop smoking before you have finished the whole book. As you read further your desire to smoke will gradually be reduced until it disappears entirely. Let the book do its work. Remember, all you have to do is to follow the instructions.

With the benefit of more than twenty years' feedback since the book's original publication, apart from Chapter 28 ('Timing'), this instruction to continue to smoke has caused me more frustration than any other. When I first stopped smoking, many of my friends and relatives stopped, purely because I had done it. They thought "If he can do it, anyone can." Over the years, by dropping little hints I managed to persuade the ones who hadn't stopped to realize just how nice it was to be free! When the book was first printed I gave copies to the hard core that were still puffing away. I worked on the basis that, even if it was the most boring book ever written, they would still read it, if only because it had been written by a friend. I was surprised and hurt to learn that, months later, they hadn't bothered to read it. I even discovered that the original copy I had signed and given to someone who was then my closest friend had not only been ignored but actually given away. I was hurt at the time, but I had overlooked the dreadful fear that slavery to the weed instills in the smoker. It can transcend friendship. I nearly provoked a divorce because of it. My mother once said to my wife, "Why don't you threaten to leave him if he doesn't stop smoking?" My wife said, "Because he'd leave me if I did." I'm ashamed to admit it, but I believe she was right, such is the fear that smokers suffer when confronted with the prospect of having to stop.

I now realize that many smokers don't finish the book because they feel they have got to stop smoking when they do. Some deliberately read only one line a day in order to postpone what they perceive to be the "evil" day. Now I am fully aware that many readers are only reading this book because they have had their arm twisted to do so by people that love them. Look at it this way: what have you got to lose? If you don't stop at the end of the book, you are no worse off than you are now. YOU HAVE ABSOLUTELY NOTHING TO LOSE AND SO MUCH TO GAIN!

Incidentally, if you have not smoked for a few days or weeks but are not yet sure whether you are a smoker, an ex-smoker or a non-smoker, then don't smoke while you read. In fact, you are already a non-smoker. All we have to do is to let your brain catch up with your body. By the end of the book you'll be a *happy* non-smoker.

Basically my method is the complete opposite of the so-called "normal" method of trying to stop. The "normal" method is to list the considerable disadvantages of smoking and say, "If only I can go long enough without a cigarette, eventually the desire to smoke will subside. I then might be able to enjoy life again."

On the surface, this appears to be a logical way to go about it, however, the truth is that over 95% of such quit attempts end in failure for the following reasons:

1. By focusing on the disadvantages of smoking we are addressing the wrong issue. We should be focused on why

we smoke, not why we shouldn't smoke. Smokers already know they shouldn't smoke, and if this knowledge were going to make them stop, it would have done so long ago. The real challenge is to understand the illusory reasons we do smoke, and deal with them.

2. Some of the things we use to motivate us to abstain do make us want to quit, but some of them also make us want to smoke. This sounds illogical but it isn't. Take the biggest reason that smokers want to stop: health. If you see an anti-smoking commercial highlighting the dangers of smoking, for example showing a throat cancer sufferer continuing to smoke through a hole in her throat, it provokes an emotional response based around the fear and anxiety that the same might happen to you. This in turn creates stress and the smoker's first response to stress is to want to light a cigarette. This is why so many quit smoking campaigns make it harder, not easier, for smokers to stop.

3. It perpetuates the myth that the smoker is sacrificing something or depriving himself of something when he stops. This sense of deprivation makes us feel miserable and vulnerable, which in turn makes the cigarette appear desirable. We have to use willpower not to give in to this desire and we enter that familiar cycle of wanting to smoke but not being allowed to. This deepens the misery and stress, which of course further heightens the desire to smoke, and so it continues until we can eventually take no more, admit defeat and light up. The problem here is not the cigarette itself, but the desire to smoke. If the smoker retains the desire to smoke then so long as he is not smoking, he will be miserable. This poor soul doesn't ever become a true non-smoker, but remains forever a smoker who is not allowed to smoke, a bit like the AA "dry drunk."

The EASYWAY is basically this: to forget, for a time, the reasons we want to stop, to turn to face the cigarette and to ask ourselves the following questions:

1. What does the cigarette really do for me?
2. Do I really enjoy it?
3. Do I really need to go through life paying through the nose just to stick these things in my mouth and suffocate myself?

The beautiful truth is that it does absolutely nothing for you at all. Let me make it quite clear, I do not mean that the disadvantages of being a smoker outweigh the advantages; all smokers know that all their lives. I mean there are NO advantages whatsoever to smoking. The only benefit it ever had was a dubious one to begin with, as a social lubricant, and that's long gone. Nowadays even smokers themselves regard it as antisocial.

All smokers attempt to rationalize why they smoke but all of the reasons we use to justify our smoking are excuses or based on myths, fallacies and illusions.

The first thing we are going to do is to address and remove these myths, fallacies and illusions. In fact, you will quickly realize that there is nothing to give up. Not only is there nothing to give up, but there are many marvelous positive gains to be had from becoming a non-smoker, and health and money are just two of these gains. Once the illusion that life will never be quite as enjoyable without the cigarette is removed, once you realize that not only is life just as enjoyable without it but infinitely more so, once the feeling of being deprived or of missing out is eradicated, then we can reconsider health and money— and the dozens of other amazingly positive reasons for stopping smoking. These realizations will become powerful additional aids to help you achieve what every smoker really wants—to enjoy the whole of your life free from the slavery of smoking.

CHAPTER 3

WHY IS IT DIFFICULT TO STOP?

As I explained earlier, I got interested in this subject because of my own addiction. When I finally stopped smoking, it was like magic. When I had tried to stop previously there were weeks of dark depression. There would be odd days when I was comparatively cheerful but the next day I would invariably sink back into the misery and depression. It was like clawing your way out of a slippery pit—you feel that you are nearing the top; you can see the sunshine—and then find yourself sliding back down again. Eventually, to end the misery, you light a cigarette. It tastes awful, makes you even more depressed and you try to work out why you keep doing this to yourself. The first thing you want to do is to quit again.

One of the questions we ask smokers prior to a consultation is "Do you want to stop smoking?" In a way it is a needless question. All smokers, including our friends in the smoker's rights groups, would love to stop smoking. If you say to even the hardest of hardcore smokers , "If you could go back to the time before you got hooked, with the knowledge you have now, would you have started smoking?" "NO WAY!" is the reply.

Say to the most confirmed smoker—someone who doesn't think that smoking injures their health, who is not worried about the social stigma and who can afford it (there aren't many around these days)—"Do you encourage your children to smoke?" "NO WAY!" is again the reply.

All smokers intuitively feel that something evil has taken possession of them. In the early days it was a question of "I'm going to stop, but not today, maybe tomorrow." Eventually we get to the stage where we think that we either don't have the required amount of willpower or that there is something inherently so enjoyable about smoking that we can't enjoy life without cigarettes.

As I said previously, the problem is not explaining why it is easy to stop; *it's understanding why we believe it has to be so difficult*. In fact, the real challenge is to explain why anybody smokes in the first place and why, at one time, over 60% of the adult population were smoking.

The whole business of smoking is an extraordinary enigma. The only reason we begin to smoke is because of the influence of the thousands of people already doing it. Yet every one of them wishes they had never started in the first place. As youngsters, we cannot quite believe they are not enjoying it. We associate smoking with adulthood and growing up, which all teenagers aspire to do. We work hard to learn to smoke and become hooked ourselves. We then spend the rest of our smoking lives trying to stop and telling our own children not to take it up in the first place.

We also spend the rest of our lives paying through the nose for what we now perceive to be our own stupidity. The average pack-a-day smoker in the US has to earn $250,000 in their lifetime to finance their addiction. It wouldn't be so bad if we just threw that money out with the garbage, but we use it to systematically suffocate ourselves, congest our lungs with cancer-triggering tars and to poison every cell of our bodies with the hundreds of toxic chemicals contained in tobacco smoke. Every day we increasingly starve every muscle and organ of oxygen, so that we become more and more lethargic. We sentence ourselves to a lifetime of bad breath, stained teeth, filthy ashtrays, vile-smelling hair, clothes and furniture and standing alone outside, banished to the sidewalks even in sub-zero temperatures. It is a lifetime of slavery. We spend the majority of our lives in situations where we can't smoke, feeling deprived. We are forever seeking opportunities to smoke, planning our next cigarette, building our day around the next occasion when we'll be able to light up. And when we *are* allowed to smoke, we wish we didn't have to. We look at the cigarette and we think, "Why am I doing this?"

What sort of hobby or pastime or pleasure or habit is it that when you are doing it you wish you weren't, and that only seems desirable when you are not doing it? It's a lifetime of being treated by the bulk of society (sometimes our own family included) like some sort of leper and, worst of all, living with a profound sense of self-disgust. The smoker despises himself and his inability to control this one aspect of his life - every time the government needs to balance its books and slaps another couple of dollars on a carton, every Great American Smokeout, every time we glance at a pack and see the health warning, every time we see an anti-smoking ad on TV, every time we feel short of breath or a pain in the chest, every time we are the only smoker in a group full of non-smokers. And what do we get out of it? ABSOLUTELY NOTHING! Pleasure? Enjoyment? Relaxation? A prop? A boost? If any of these things were true, smokers would be happier and more relaxed than non-smokers.

As I have said, the real challenge is not to explain why smokers perceive stopping as difficult, but to explain why anybody does it at all.

You are probably saying, "That's all very well. I know this, but once you are hooked on cigarettes it is very difficult to stop smoking." But *why* is it so difficult, and why do we "have to" keep doing it? Smokers search for the answers to these questions all of their lives.

Some say it is because of the terrible physical withdrawal symptoms. In fact, the actual withdrawal symptoms from nicotine are so mild (see Chapter 6) that most smokers go through their whole smoking lives without ever realizing they are drug addicts.

Some say that it's the taste and smell of cigarettes that keep us smoking. Nothing could be further from the truth. They are filthy, disgusting objects. Ask any smoker who suffers from the illusion that he enjoys the taste if, when he can't get his brand, he stops smoking. Smokers would rather smoke old rope than not smoke at all. I enjoy the taste of lobster but I never got to the stage where I had to have twenty lobsters with me everywhere I went. The truth is that we smoke *despite* the smell and taste of cigarettes, not because of it.

Some search for deep psychological reasons to rationalize why they smoke; for example, the Freudian analysis of the cigarette as a substitute for a mother's breast. This sounds good, but doesn't make much sense when you analyze it. Most kids start smoking to demonstrate that they are adults and no longer tied to the mother's apron strings, which is the exact opposite of wanting a substitute for the breast. If it were true that cigarettes provided a feeling of safety and security then everyone would smoke. After all, we all have the same human needs to feel safe, secure and loved.

Some argue the reverse, that the cigarette is a badge of adulthood and independence. Again, the opposite is closer to the truth. How do we demonstrate our independence by becoming dependent on a drug that enslaves us?

Some say, "It is something to do with my hands!" So, why light it?

"It is oral satisfaction." So, why light it?

"It is the feeling of the smoke going into my lungs." An awful feeling—replacing oxygen with poison—it is called suffocation.

Many believe that smoking relieves boredom but if that were true, then smokers would never be bored. Are smokers saying that there is a magic ingredient in tobacco that is a genuine medical cure for boredom? And if we smoke to relieve boredom, then why do we also smoke when we are not bored? What the smoker is really saying here is that the cigarette creates a distraction that allows us, for a moment or two, to forget we are bored.

But the same smoker will argue that the cigarette helps them to concentrate. There is a contradiction here. When we need to concentrate, we remove distractions, we don't create them. So is the cigarette a distraction or does it remove distractions? It can't do both. How is it possible that a drug which provides a distraction at 9:00 a.m. can miraculously remove distractions at 9:30 a.m.? It can't.

And there is another contradiction too. Smokers claim that the cigarette relaxes them and helps them to handle stressful situations. But they also claim that it helps them get going in the morning, and that it gives them a boost. How can a drug that relaxes you or relieves stress also stimulate you? This contradiction illustrates the truth about smoking. The cigarette just doesn't do any of the things we tell ourselves it does.

If cigarettes relaxed us and helped to relieve stress then smokers would be more relaxed and less stressed than non-smokers.

If cigarettes helped us to get going and helped us concentrate, then smokers would be more energetic and would enjoy enhanced brain function. All athletes would be smokers, as would all university professors and Nobel Prize winners. It would be mandatory for people in stressful professions, like air traffic controllers and surgeons, to smoke. Do you smell what I smell?

For thirty-three years my excuse was that it relaxed me, and gave me confidence and courage. I also knew it was killing me and costing me a fortune. Why didn't I go to my doctor and ask him for something to relax me and give me courage and confidence? I didn't in case he did. It wasn't my reason; it was my excuse.

Some say they do it for social reasons, because their friends do it. That may hold water when we are twelve or thirteen, just starting out, but it doesn't make sense when we are fully-grown, independent adults.

Most smokers who think about it eventually come to the conclusion that it is just a habit. This is not really an explanation but, having discounted all the rational explanations it appears to be the only excuse that makes sense. Unfortunately, when we scratch the surface, this explanation is equally illogical. We make and break habits every day of our lives, and some of them are very enjoyable. We have been brainwashed into believing that smoking is a habit, and that habits are hard to break. Are habits hard to break? In the UK we drive on the left side of the road. Yet when we travel to the US I need to drive on the right. So I break my UK driving "habit" and immediately acquire a new "habit" with hardly any aggravation whatsoever. The change causes me no mental anguish or physical torture. I don't miss driving on the left or develop a craving to do so. It is clearly a fallacy that habits are hard to break. We do it every day with no bother whatsoever.

So why do we find it difficult to break a "habit" that tastes awful, that kills us, costs us a fortune, that is filthy and disgusting and that we would love to break anyway, when all we need to do is to stop doing it? The answer is that smoking is not a habit: IT IS NICOTINE ADDICTION! Perhaps you feel this explanation explains why it *is* difficult to "give up." It certainly explains why so many smokers believe that it has to be difficult. This misconception arises because most smokers do not understand drug addiction and it persists because they have been brainwashed into believing that they get some genuine pleasure or crutch from smoking. They therefore believe that they are making a genuine sacrifice when they quit.

The beautiful truth is that once you understand nicotine addiction and the real reasons you smoke it is easy to stop smoking. A few weeks from now the only mystery will be why you found it necessary to smoke for as long as you have, and why you cannot persuade other smokers of HOW NICE IT IS TO BE A NON-SMOKER!

CHAPTER 4

THE SINISTER TRAP

Smoking is the most subtle, sinister trap that man and nature have ever combined to devise. What or who gets us into the trap in the first place? The thousands who have already fallen into it. They even warn us not to start. That smoking is a filthy, disgusting habit that will eventually destroy us and cost us a fortune, but still we cannot believe that they are not enjoying it. One of the most tragic aspects of smoking is how hard we have to work in order to become hooked.

It is the only trap in nature which has no lure, no bait. What springs the trap is not that cigarettes taste so marvelous; it's that they taste so awful. If that first cigarette tasted wonderful, alarm bells would ring and, as intelligent human beings, we could then understand why so many get hooked and spend the rest of their lives smoking. But because that first cigarette tastes so awful, our young minds are reassured that we could never become hooked on something so disgusting, and we think that because we are not enjoying them we can stop whenever we want to. But by that stage we are already hooked.

Nicotine is the only drug in nature that has the opposite effect to that which is desired. Boys usually start because they want to appear tough or cool—like Mel Gibson in *Lethal Weapon* or Bruce Willis in the *Die Hard* movies. In reality, tough is the last thing you feel when smoking your first cigarette. You dare not inhale, and if you do, you start to feel dizzy, then sick—usually within seconds. All you want to do is get away from the other boys and throw the filthy things away. We don't even need the health warnings. Our bodies tell us in no uncertain terms—GET THIS POISON OUT OF ME!

With girls or young women, the aim is to be the sophisticated modern young lady. We have all seen them taking little drags on a cigarette, looking absolutely ridiculous. Trying to copy Lindsay Lohan, Britney Spears, Julia Roberts or Sarah Jessica Parker, or in years gone by, Bette Davis or Marlene Dietrich—epitomes of successful, attractive women.

By the time the boys have learned to look tough and the girls sophisticated, they wish they had never started in the first place. Actually, I'm now of the view that no woman looks sophisticated when they smoke. Notice how pictures of these beautiful, glamorous smokers never show them actually smoking, but just holding the lit cigarette. It seems to me that there is no intermediate stage between the obvious beginner and the wrinkled, pinched look of a hardcore smoker.

After we get hooked we then spend the rest of our lives trying to justify to ourselves why we do it, telling our children not to get caught in the trap and, at odd times trying to escape ourselves.

The trap is so designed that we only try to stop when we have stress in our lives, whether it be health, shortage of money or being made to feel like a leper and a criminal.

Because smokers associate stress relief with cigarettes, these stressful situations that motivate us to quit also make us want to smoke. As soon as we stop, we have more stress in our lives because we want a cigarette but can't have one. Previously, we relied on the cigarette to relieve stress but now we must do without.

After a few hours or days of torture we decide that we have picked the wrong time to quit. We must wait for a period when we have less stress, but as soon as we have less stress, our reasons for stopping vanish. Of course, that perfectly stress-free time never arrives. As we leave the protection of our parents, the natural process is to find a partner, build a family and a career and so on. We perceive these things to be stressful but they are really just part of growing up and becoming adults. We tend to confuse responsibility with stress. The truth is that the most stressful period of our lives is childhood and early adolescence. This is the period of our lives when everything is new and unknown, when our world is going through profound and constant change over which we have little or no control. Yet during this time of tremendous change and stress, we are perfectly able to handle it without cigarettes or any other false props or drugs.

Smokers' lives are significantly more stressful than non-smokers'. This is because tobacco does not relax you or relieve stress, as the brainwashing would have you believe. Just the reverse: smoking actually causes you to become more nervous, stressed and far less relaxed than non-smokers. You don't need a degree in biochemistry to know this, just look around—it's plain to see.

The whole business of smoking is like wandering into a giant maze. As we enter the maze our minds become misted up and clouded, and we spend the rest of our lives trying to find our way back out.

I spent thirty-three years trying to escape from that maze. Like all smokers, I couldn't understand it. However, due to a combination of unusual circumstances, none of which reflect any credit on me, I wanted to know why previously it had been so desperately difficult to stop and yet, when I did finally quit, it was not only easy but enjoyable.

Since stopping smoking, my hobby and later my life's work has been to try to solve the many conundrums associated with smoking. It is a complex and fascinating puzzle and, like the Rubik's Cube, practically impossible to solve without assistance. However, like all complicated puzzles, if you have an instruction manual and know the solution, it is easy! I have the solution to stopping smoking easily and this book is your instruction manual. I will lead you out of the maze and ensure that you never wander into it again. All you have to do is *follow the instructions*. This means exactly what it says. If you don't follow an instruction, then in effect you take a wrong turn in trying to escape from the maze. One wrong turn renders the rest of the instructions meaningless.

Let me be very clear about this: any smoker can find it easy to stop smoking, but first we need to establish the facts. No, I do not mean statistics about lung cancer, heart disease and the many other conditions caused by smoking. You are already aware of this information and if it was going to stop you from smoking, it would have done so years ago. I mean, why do we find it difficult to stop? In order to answer this question we first need to know why we smoke.

CHAPTER 5

WHY WE SMOKE

Most of us started smoking for largely stupid reasons, usually involving a degree of peer pressure, but once we become aware that we're hooked, why do we carry on smoking?

No smoker truly understands why he or she smokes. If they did, they would stop immediately and effortlessly. I have asked this question of thousands of smokers during my consultations. The correct answer is the same for all smokers, but the variety of replies is infinite. All smokers know in their heart of hearts that they have been scammed. They know that they had no need to smoke before they became hooked. Most of them can remember that their first cigarette tasted awful and that they had to work hard to tolerate the disgusting smell and taste. Smokers are intelligent, rational human beings. They know that they are taking enormous risks with their health and their family's future and that they spend a fortune on cigarettes in their lifetime. Therefore it is necessary for them to develop a rational explanation to justify their smoking.

The actual reason why smokers continue to smoke is a subtle combination of the factors I will elaborate on in the next two chapters. They are:

1. NICOTINE ADDICTION
2. BRAINWASHING

CHAPTER 6

NICOTINE ADDICTION

Nicotine, a colorless, oily compound, is the drug contained in tobacco that addicts the smoker. It is the most addictive drug known to mankind, and it can take just one cigarette to become hooked. One drag of one cigarette is enough for former smokers to get hooked again.

Every drag of a cigarette delivers, via the lungs to the brain, a small dose of nicotine that acts more rapidly than the dose of heroin the addict injects into his veins. In fact, this comparison is one that the tobacco companies themselves use. In an internal memorandum dated 1971, a Philip Morris executive wrote: *"The cigarette should be conceived not as a product but as a package. The product is nicotine. Think of the cigarette pack as a storage container for a day's supply of nicotine. Think of a cigarette as a dispenser for a dose unit of nicotine."*

Nicotine is a very fast-acting drug, which sounds frightening, but is actually good news because it means that it not only enters the body quickly but also leaves the body quickly. Immediately after putting out a cigarette, nicotine levels begin to fall. There is enough nicotine in each cigarette to make the average smoker feel the need to smoke about every forty-five minutes. Incidentally, this explains why most smokers smoke around twenty cigarettes per day.

As soon as the smoker puts out the cigarette, the nicotine starts to leave the body and the smoker goes into withdrawal.

At this point I must dispel a common illusion that smokers have about withdrawal. Most believe that withdrawal pangs are the terrible trauma that is experienced when a smoker isn't able to smoke, or is attempting to quit. This is not true. These pangs are, in fact, mainly mental and are caused by the illusion that the smoker is depriving himself of his pleasure or crutch.

The actual pangs of withdrawal from nicotine are so slight that most smokers have lived and died without even realizing they are drug addicts. Fortunately it is an easy drug to kick, once you understand the nature of the addiction and accept that you are, in fact, addicted. This point was quite a revelation when this book was first published. Now it is universally accepted.

There is no physical pain in the withdrawal from nicotine. It is merely a slightly empty, restless feeling, the feeling that something isn't quite right, or that something is missing, which is why many smokers think it is a feeling of needing something to do with their hands. If it is prolonged, the smoker becomes increasingly anxious, insecure, agitated and irritable. It is like hunger—for a poison, NICOTINE.

Within seven seconds of lighting up the nicotine contained in that cigarette reaches the brain and the "craving" ends, along with the feelings of anxiety and irritability, resulting in the feeling of relaxation and security that the cigarette appears to give to the smoker. This is an illusion though. The feeling of "relief" is really just the ending of the state of tension that was created by the previous cigarette.

In the early days, this whole process of withdrawal and relief when replenishment takes place is so slight that we are not even aware that it is taking place. When we begin to smoke regularly we think it is either because we've come to enjoy it or that we have got into the "habit." The truth is that we're already hooked. We don't realize it, but it's like a little nicotine monster has taken up residence inside us and its appetite is slowly but surely growing.

All smokers start smoking for a variety of stupid reasons. But the only reason why anybody continues to smoke, whether they are a "casual" or heavy smoker, is to feed that metaphorical "little monster."

This, for me, is the saddest thing about smoking: the only "enjoyment" a smoker gets from a cigarette is temporary relief from the discomfort created by the previous one. All the smoker is looking for is the state of peace, tranquility and confidence that they had before they started smoking in the first place.

You know that feeling when a neighbor's burglar alarm has been ringing all day, or there has been some other minor, persistent aggravation? The noise suddenly stops and we experience a wonderful feeling of peace and tranquility. Actually, this peace is something of an illusion. All that has really happened is that the aggravation has disappeared and everything has returned to normal. What we are really enjoying is not the feeling of normality, but the ending of the aggravation.

Before we start smoking, our bodies and our lives are complete. We then force nicotine into our body by smoking our first cigarette. When we put that first cigarette out, the nicotine begins to leaves the body and is replaced by that barely noticeable feeling of a slight emptiness, a bit like hunger. This is nicotine withdrawal—my metaphorical "little monster." If we smoke again, the nicotine is replaced, the slight emptiness disappears and is replaced by a feeling of relaxation, satisfaction and confidence, (i.e., a feeling of normality). But the nicotine from the second cigarette also leaves the body, so the empty feeling returns. So we need to light another cigarette to remove that feeling and once again feel normal. And so the smoker's cycle of withdrawal and replenishment begins. It's a lifelong chain of attempts to relieve the slight aggravation caused by withdrawal and to once again feel normal.

The whole business of smoking is like forcing yourself to wear tight shoes just to get the pleasure of taking them off.

This process is very visible and obvious to non-smokers. It's clear to them that their smoking friends and colleagues aren't happier or less stressed or more relaxed than non-smokers when they smoke. Rather, it's that smokers are *less* happy, *more* stressed and *less* relaxed when they *can't* smoke.

Because non-smokers see smoking this way, they correctly perceive no advantages to smoking. As a consequence, they have no desire to smoke. With no desire to do something, it takes no willpower not to do it.

There are three main reasons why smokers find it difficult to perceive cigarettes in this way.

1. From birth we have been exposed to massive brainwashing telling us that smokers receive immense pleasure from smoking or that it provides a crutch to help us cope with stress. We just can't believe that smokers would spend huge sums of money and take horrendous risks with their health to do something that doesn't give them anything.

2. Because physical withdrawal from nicotine is so mild, just a slightly empty, insecure feeling, we don't think of cigarettes in the same way as we think of other drugs. Because smokers are in withdrawal whenever they are not smoking,

they come to perceive the state of withdrawal as "normal"; inseparable in our minds from hunger or mild stress.

3. However the main reason that smokers fail to see smoking in its true light is because it works back to front. It's when you are *not* smoking that you suffer that empty feeling. When you light up, it disappears, and we give the cigarette the credit for this. What we forget is that withdrawing from the previous cigarette created that empty feeling in the first place! This is the illusion of pleasure we associate with smoking. We only acknowledge the boost the cigarette gives us. What we don't acknowledge is that the previous cigarette created the need for the boost back to normal in the first place. Of course, non-smokers don't need this illusory boost because they didn't get the empty feeling caused by withdrawing from the previous cigarette to begin with.

It is our inability to understand this reverse process that can make it difficult to kick this or any other drug. Fortunately, once you understand the process, it's easy. Picture the panic of a heroin addict who has not been able to shoot up for several hours or days. Now picture the relief when that addict can finally plunge a hypodermic needle into his vein. If you witnessed such a scene, would you conclude that shooting up with heroin relieves panic, or would you think that heroin withdrawal *creates* it? Non-heroin addicts don't suffer that panic feeling when they can't shoot up. The heroin doesn't relieve the symptoms of panic; withdrawing from the previous dose caused them.

Equally, non-smokers don't get the empty feeling of needing a cigarette or start to panic when they can't smoke. The cigarette *causes* those symptoms and the next one temporarily relieves them to provide the illusion of pleasure or the illusion of relief.

Smokers talk about cigarettes relaxing them and giving satisfaction. But how can you even notice being relaxed unless you were tense in the first place? How can we suddenly feel satisfied unless you were previously dissatisfied? Why don't non-smokers suffer from this state of tension and dissatisfaction? Why is it that after a meal, when non-smokers are completely relaxed and happy, smokers are tense and edgy—until they have fed that little nicotine monster?

Forgive me if I dwell on this subject for a moment. The main reason that smokers find it difficult to quit is that they believe that they are giving up a genuine pleasure or crutch. It is absolutely essential to understand that there is nothing to "give up."

The best way to understand the subtleties of the nicotine trap is to compare it with eating. If we are in the habit of eating at set times during the day, we don't get hungry between meals. Only if the meal is delayed are we aware of being hungry, and even then, there is no physical pain, just an empty, slightly insecure feeling which we know as: "I need to eat." And the process of satisfying our hunger can be very enjoyable indeed.

Smoking appears on the surface to be almost identical. The empty, insecure feeling we know as wanting or "needing" a cigarette is almost identical to a hunger for food. Like hunger, there is no physical pain and the sensation is so slight that we are not even aware of it for much of the day. It's only when we want to smoke but aren't allowed to do so—the equivalent of the meal being delayed—that we become aware of any discomfort. When we do light up the discomfort ends and we once again feel normal.

Incidentally, this is also why some smokers believe that the cigarette works as an appetite suppressant. Smoking doesn't suppress the appetite; it's just that withdrawal feels like hunger (I discuss this in more detail in Chapter 30, Will I Put On Weight?).

It is this superficial similarity between smoking and eating which fools smokers into believing they sometimes get a genuine pleasure or crutch when they smoke. Sadly, the truth is that all they have done is to remove the slight feeling of discomfort caused by the previous cigarette. Some smokers find it difficult to accept that there is no pleasure or crutch whatsoever to smoking. Some argue: "How can you say there is no crutch? You tell me when I light up that I'll remove the feeling of discomfort." But the point is that the non-smoker didn't feel any discomfort to begin with.

Although eating and smoking appear to be very similar, in fact they are exact opposites:

1. You eat to survive and to be healthy, whereas tobacco is the biggest cause of preventable death and disease in the history of Western civilization.

2. Food genuinely tastes good, and eating can be a genuinely pleasant experience, whereas smoking involves ingesting extremely toxic fumes and is known to cause depression, anxiety and panic disorders.

3. Eating doesn't create hunger, it genuinely relieves it. Cigarettes don't satisfy the "hunger" to smoke, they create and perpetuate it.

On the subject of hunger, this is an opportune moment to dispel another common myth about smoking, that smoking is a habit, a point I have touched on previously. Is eating a habit? If you think so, try breaking it completely! To describe eating as a habit would be the same as describing breathing as a habit. Both are essential for survival. It is true that different people are in the habit of satisfying their hunger at different times and with different types of food. But eating itself is not a habit. Neither is smoking. The only reason any smoker lights a cigarette is to try to end the slightly empty, insecure hunger-like feeling that was created by the nicotine contained in the previous cigarette. It is true that different smokers are in the habit of trying to relieve their withdrawal pangs at different times and with different brands, but smoking itself is not a habit.

Society continues to refer to smoking as a "habit" and so in this book, for convenience, I sometimes also refer to the "habit." However, be constantly aware that smoking is *not* habit, IT IS DRUG ADDICTION!

When we start to smoke we force our body to learn to cope with the poisons along with the disgusting smell and taste. Before we know it, we are not only buying them regularly but we *have* to have them. If we don't, we get anxious and panic sets in. Over time we tend to need to smoke more and more.

This is because, as with all drugs, the body creates some immunity to the effects of nicotine. We therefore need to smoke more to obtain the same effect. After quite a short period the cigarette ceases to completely relieve the withdrawal pangs created by the previous one, so that when you light a cigarette even though you do feel better, you are in fact still slightly more stressed and slightly less relaxed than you would be as a non-smoker, even when you are actually smoking the cigarette. The situation worsens because, once the cigarette is extinguished, the nicotine rapidly leaves the body, creating more withdrawal symptoms. This is why, in stressful situations, so many smokers tend to chain-smoke.

As I said, the "habit" doesn't exist. The real reason every smoker keeps smoking is to feed that "little monster" he has created. The monster tends to need feeding in certain situations and we come to associate these occasions (or a combination of them) with smoking. The "big four" smoking occasions are:

BOREDOM & CONCENTRATION—two complete opposites!

STRESS & RELAXATION—two complete opposites!

How can a drug that relieves boredom by providing a distraction suddenly help you concentrate when you need to remove distractions? It's the same drug. It can't do both things because they are opposites.

The truth is that smoking doesn't do any of the things that, as smokers, we must tell ourselves it does. If smoking REALLY relieved boredom, aided concentration, relaxed us and got us ready for action, then smokers would be more engaged, energetic, better able to concentrate and less stressed than non-smokers. Even smokers will admit that this is not the case, and the world of science agrees—research shows smokers to have lower energy levels, more problems concentrating and much higher levels of stress than non-smokers.

Apart from being a drug (albeit one with no noticeable "high"), nicotine is also a powerful poison and tiny amounts are used in many commercial insecticides. If the nicotine content of just one cigarette were injected directly into your bloodstream, it would kill you. In fact, tobacco contains hundreds of poisons, including benzene, polonium and cyanide. This should not come as a surprise as the tobacco plant is from the same family as the deadly nightshade. In addition, many cigarettes also contain toxic additives such as ammonia and formaldehyde.

In case you have visions of switching to a pipe or cigars, I should make it quite clear that the content of this book applies to all tobacco. Indeed nicotine is so toxic that it is hard to see any reason to consume any product containing it, including nicotine gum, patches, tabs, e-cigarettes, nasal sprays, lozenges, inhalators, chewing tobacco, and Snus (orally taken tobacco common in Scandinavia and just launched in the US, where it seems to be geared towards attracting young people).

No species on earth, from the lowest amoeba or worm upwards, can survive without knowing the difference between food and poison.

The human body is by far the most sophisticated machine on the planet. Over millions of years, our minds and bodies have developed techniques for distinguishing between food and poison and fail-safe methods for rejecting the latter.

All human beings are averse to the smell and taste of tobacco until they become hooked. We don't even need the health warnings to know that tobacco is poisonous. We need only to listen to our bodies. If you blow smoke into the face of any animal, it will instinctively cough and splutter in an attempt to expel the poison.

When we smoked our first cigarette, for most of us inhaling resulted in a coughing fit. If we managed to smoke the whole thing, we most likely experienced dizziness or nausea. These symptoms were our body's way of telling us: "YOU ARE FEEDING ME POISON. STOP IT." This is the key moment that often decides our future: whether we become smokers or not. It is a fallacy that weak and weak-willed people become smokers. Smokers need to be strong and strong-willed to endure the process of learning to smoke. The lucky ones are those who find that first cigarette so repulsive that they cannot go through this process of learning to tolerate tobacco smoke; physically their lungs cannot cope with it, and they avoid the trap.

To me this is the most tragic part of the whole business. How hard we have to work to become hooked in the first place! Ironically, this is why it is difficult to get teenagers to quit. Because they still find cigarettes and smoking distasteful, they refuse to believe that they can get hooked. They believe they can stop whenever they want to. Sadly, by this stage, they are already addicted. Why do they not learn from us? Then again, why did we not learn from our parents?

Some smokers believe they enjoy the taste and smell of the tobacco. This, like so much else with respect to smoking, is an illusion. What we are actually doing when we learn to smoke is teaching our bodies to become desensitized to the disgusting smell and taste in order to get our fix.

Ask a smoker who believes he smokes because he enjoys the smell and taste of tobacco, "If you cannot get your normal brand of cigarette, do you abstain?" No way. A smoker will smoke anything rather than abstain. Smokers prefer their own brands because they have taught themselves to tolerate the smell and taste, but if their brand isn't available a smoker will smoke any brand in order to get his fix. This is why smokers who at first find roll-ups, cigars, menthols or pipes absolutely disgusting, over time can learn to "like" or, more accurately, tolerate them.

Smokers will even keep smoking through colds, flu, sore throats, bronchitis and emphysema. Taste, smell and "enjoyment" have nothing to do with it. If it did, no one would smoke more than one cigarette. There are even thousands of people hooked on nicotine chewing gum which tastes disgusting, and many of them are also still smoking.

During our seminars some smokers find it alarming to realize that they are drug addicts and think that this will make it even more difficult to stop. In fact, it is very good news for two important reasons:

1. Most of us carry on smoking because, although we know that the disadvantages of smoking outweigh the advantages, we believe that there is something intrinsically enjoyable or special that the cigarette gives us. We feel that after we stop smoking there will be a "void," that our life will never be quite the same. This is an illusion, as I will demonstrate. The fact is that the cigarette gives you nothing.

2. Although it is a highly addictive drug because of the speed with which it hooks you, ironically, you are never badly hooked on the drug itself. Because it is so fast-acting it also leaves the body very quickly. Eight hours after putting out a cigarette, you are 97% nicotine-free. After just three days of not smoking, you are 100% nicotine-free.

You will ask, quite rightly, why if this is the case, so many smokers find it so difficult to stop, and suffer through months of torture? Why do so many spend the rest of their lives craving cigarettes at odd times, even years after they have become 100% nicotine-free?

The answer is the second component to the smoking puzzle—the brainwashing. Breaking the physical addiction and getting through the chemical withdrawal is fast and easy to cope with. In fact, smokers cope with withdrawal their whole smoking lives and they cope with it so easily that they aren't even aware it exists.

Most smokers go all night without a cigarette. The withdrawal "pangs" do not even wake them up.

Many smokers will leave the bedroom before they light that first cigarette; many will have breakfast first. Increasingly, people don't smoke in their homes and won't have that first cigarette until they are in the car on their way to work; some won't even smoke in the car and will have their first cigarette after they arrive at work. These smokers have gone eight or maybe ten hours without a cigarette—going through withdrawal all the while, but it doesn't seem to bother them.

Nowadays many smokers will automatically refrain from smoking in the homes, or even in the presence of non-smokers. Even when I was a chain-smoker I was able to go for quite long periods without smoking and it didn't bother me in the slightest.

If physical withdrawal was as bad as the brainwashing would have us believe, how is it that we can go for such long periods of time without even noticing it?

Smokers have the illusion that they only suffer from withdrawal when they try to quit. In fact, smokers suffer withdrawal their entire smoking lives. It's what makes them reach for their next cigarette. It's just that this withdrawal is so slight that we don't realize we're experiencing it. Over time, we begin to perceive the smoker's more-or-less permanent state of mild withdrawal as "normal."

While it is very, very mild, physical withdrawal from nicotine does exist—as I said, we experience it every time we put out a cigarette—but it is not the main problem. It just acts as a catalyst to confuse us over the real problem: the brainwashing.

It may be of some consolation to older and heavier smokers to know that it is just as easy for them to stop as it is for so-called "casual" smokers. In some respects, it's even easier because heavier smokers tend not to have any illusions that they enjoy smoking whereas some very light smokers still do.

It may be of further consolation for you to know that the rumors that occasionally circulate are untrue; i.e., "Every cigarette takes five minutes off your life." The human body is an incredible machine and irrespective of how many years you have been smoking, the body bounces back quickly once you quit, provided you haven't already contracted an irreversible smoking-related condition. The recovery starts immediately after you put out your final cigarette. Within just twenty minutes your heart rate returns to normal and after twenty-four hours, the likelihood of a heart attack is reduced by half.

And it is never too late to stop. I have helped to cure many smokers in their fifties, sixties and seventies, and even a few in their eighties. All reported dramatic improvements in their health, and most of them noticed the change within a couple of days. A ninety-one-year-old woman attended a seminar with her sixty-six-year-old son. When I asked why she had decided to stop she replied: "To set an example for him." She contacted me six months later saying she felt like a young girl again.

The further the drug drags you down, the greater the relief when you quit. When I finally broke free I went from a hundred cigarettes a day to ZERO, and I didn't experience one single pang. In fact, it was actually enjoyable, even during the withdrawal period.

Think of nicotine addiction as the "little monster" I mentioned earlier. It's utterly insignificant and you can squash it like a bug. The only danger of the little monster is that it feeds the big monster—the BRAINWASHING.

CHAPTER 7

BRAINWASHING AND THE SLEEPING PARTNER

How or why do we start smoking in the first place? To understand this fully we need to examine the power of the mind and in particular, the subconscious mind or, as I call it, the "sleeping partner."

We all tend to think of ourselves as intelligent human beings making conscious decisions that dictate the path of our lives, but the truth is that most of our behavior and attitudes are determined by our surroundings, upbringing and by forces of which we are largely unaware. These forces, mostly benign, work at a sub-conscious level. As children, we absorb enormous amounts of information—good, bad, useful and utterly worthless—effortlessly and without even being aware that we are learning.

Tobacco marketing executives are well aware of the importance of the sub-conscious and the power of suggestion and they have used it for years to promote the image of smoking as normal, natural and desirable. When we are growing up we are bombarded with messages that cigarettes help us relax, concentrate and handle stress. We form the belief that cigarettes are special, precious things and that we are somehow incomplete without them.

You think I exaggerate? Remember those old war movies? The dying soldier is always given a cigarette to ease him peacefully and nobly to his heroic death. What's the last request of the man facing death by a firing squad? That's right—a cigarette. The subtext running beneath this seemingly innocent request is a powerful one. What the message is really saying is, "The most precious thing on this earth, my last thought and action, will be the smoking of a cigarette." The impact of this does not register on our conscious minds, but the sleeping partner has time to absorb it.

You think that things have changed recently? Not a chance. While TV advertising for tobacco products has been banned for years, the appearance of smoking in movies and on TV continues unabated. Look at Bruce Willis in *Die Hard* or Mel Gibson in *Lethal Weapon* franchises. These movies, aimed at teenage boys, glamorize smoking in a way a TV ad never could. For two hours Mr. Willis and Mr. Gibson chain-smoke their way through a myriad of death-defying and heroic sequences. The subtext again is very simple: Even heroes need their little friend. What better way to show your cool and rebellious nature than to smoke?

Does this happen by accident, or is it part of a concerted strategy by tobacco companies to promote smoking to teenagers as cool, rebellious and desirable? I'm not a conspiracy theorist but it's obvious to me that if you are in a business where 5 million of your customers die every year, you need to replace them somehow. Given that over 90% of smokers start before their eighteenth birthday, it makes sense to market to as young a demographic as possible, without being seen to be doing so.

As a demonstration of the tobacco industry's success in promoting to children, for years the American tobacco giant RJ Reynolds ran a campaign based on a kid's cartoon character, Joe Camel. Joe Camel took RJR's market share among smokers under eighteen years old from 0.5% to 32.8% in three years. In research published in the *Journal of the American Medical Association*, over 90% of six-year-olds matched the Joe Camel character with a cigarette. According to the same research, for a time, Joe Camel was as well known as Mickey Mouse among American pre-schoolers.

And TV is no better than cinema. I recently watched an episode of the otherwise wonderful *West Wing*. Martin Sheen's character, the president of the US, when faced with a difficult decision in a stressful situation, wanders to his private study and sitting alone with the enormous burdens of his office, lights a cigarette. Once again the message being promoted: Smoking relieves stress. Even the most powerful man in the world needs his little crutch.

Think about it, what better ad could you have than actors and actresses we love and admire smoking on-screen? John Travolta, Al Pacino, Clint Eastwood, Bruce Willis, Sean Penn, Julia Roberts, Nicole Kidman, Nicolas Cage, Matt Damon, Humphrey Bogart, Lauren Bacall, Marlene Dietrich, Leonardo di Caprio, Gwyneth Paltrow…the list is endless.

Who knows whether Hollywood continues to benefit financially from working with the tobacco companies to promote smoking (though this has unquestionably been the case in years gone by) but every time an actor lights up in a movie aimed at kids, the message that smoking is normal, desirable and glamorous is reinforced. That message is filed away in the sub-conscious and the cumulative impact of it being repeated thousands upon thousands of times during a child's formative years builds a desire for kids to experiment. Perhaps that's why even today, 75% of movies rated G, PG and PG-13 feature smoking in them. Unfortunately, nicotine is so addictive that experimentation all too often leads to addiction.

True, there is publicity to counter this brainwashing, but it's a case of too little, too late. Anti-smoking campaigns fail to effectively reverse the brainwashing promoting cigarettes and smoking for two key reasons. Firstly, they tend to feature sick, and therefore older smokers. Youngsters just don't identify with a sixty-year-old woman smoking through a tracheotomy. Anyway, which teenager starts smoking with the intention of smoking for the rest of their lives? Do you think alcoholics mean to become alcoholics? Teenagers believe that they could never get hooked on cigarettes and that they could quit at any time, if they wanted to. So why would an ad featuring someone with whom they cannot identify, resonate with them? Secondly, the campaigns come too late, after the teenager has already become a smoker. As with every addiction or condition, prevention is better than cure. The truth is that these campaigns make little or no difference to children thinking about taking up smoking, or smokers wanting to quit.

The trap is the same today as when Sir Walter Raleigh fell into it. All the anti-smoking campaigns do is confuse the issue. The challenge is not so much to counter the brainwashing as it is to ensure that our children aren't subjected to it in the first place.

For an example of the power of the brainwashing to which the smoker is subjected, and the fear that it creates, one need look no further than the issue closest—in more ways than one—to the smoker's heart. Although we are acutely aware of the health risks associated with smoking, and for the most part don't argue or debate those risks, smokers point to the exceptions to the rule. Every smoker knows of an Uncle Fred who smoked two packs a day, never had a day's illness in his life, and lived to eighty. We ignore the fact that for every Uncle Fred, there is a Peter Jennings, Humphrey Bogart, Steve McQueen, George Harrison, Betty Grable, Ed Sullivan, Johnny Carson, Lucille Ball, Bette Davis or Errol Flynn. Every day nearly 1,500 Americans die of smoking-related causes. We also ignore the fact that Uncle Fred might still be alive if he hadn't been a smoker.

I highlight this capacity for self-delusion not to try to make you feel bad—I was the worst of the lot when I was a smoker—but to illustrate the extent to which we are brainwashed into searching for any scrap of information that allows us to continue to justify our smoking.

We're even brainwashed into minimizing the problems that smoking creates in favor of demonizing other social issues, far less harmful than tobacco. As a society we are rightly concerned about crack or heroin addiction, yet actual deaths from these drugs are a small fraction of the annual tobacco-related deaths. In 2003, glue sniffing, heroin use and marijuana use caused around 3,000 deaths in the US. Tragic as those deaths indisputably are, they don't compare to the 450,000 deaths caused by tobacco.

Marijuana is often labeled as a "gateway" drug, but over 80% of alcoholics are smokers and I have yet to meet a heroin addict who isn't a smoker. If there is a gateway drug it is nicotine.

Governments around the world have a love/hate relationship with tobacco. On the one hand, governments salivate over billions in tobacco revenues but on the other hand they know that this revenue will be far outstripped by the future medical and other costs associated with smoking. So far, greed is winning the battle at the expense of smokers and their families.

One of the key challenges in becoming a happy non-smoker is to see through all this brainwashing and to recognize cigarettes for what they really are. Very early on in our smoking lives we unwittingly elevate the cigarette's importance and place it on a pedestal. There it remains for the rest of our smoking lives, unchallenged and all-powerful. We need to begin to ask some searching questions:

- Why am I doing it?
- What does the cigarette really do for me?
- Do I really need to smoke?

NO, OF COURSE YOU DON'T.

I find this brainwashing the most difficult aspect of smoking to explain. Why is it that an otherwise rational, intelligent human being becomes a complete imbecile when it comes to looking at his own addiction? It pains me to confess that out of all of the people that I have assisted in stopping smoking, I was the biggest idiot of all.

My father was a heavy smoker. He was a strong man, cut down in his prime by smoking. I can remember watching him when I was a boy; he would be coughing and spluttering in the mornings. I could see he wasn't enjoying it and it was obvious to me that something evil had possessed him. I can remember saying to my mother, "Don't ever let me become a smoker."

At the age of fifteen I was a physical-fitness fanatic. Sport was my life and I was full of energy, courage and confidence. If anybody had said to me that I would end up smoking a hundred cigarettes a day, I would have gambled my lifetime's earnings that it would not happen, and I would have given any odds that had been asked.

At the age of forty I was a physical and mental wreck. I had reached the stage where I couldn't carry out the most mundane task without first lighting up. With most smokers the triggers are the normal, mild stresses of life, like answering the telephone or socializing. I couldn't even change the TV channel on my remote without lighting up.

I knew it was killing me. There was no way I could kid my-self otherwise. But what I fail to understand is why I couldn't see what it was doing to me mentally and emotionally. It was almost jumping up and biting me on the nose. The really ridiculous thing is I never even suffered the illusion that I enjoyed smok-ing. I smoked because I thought it helped me to concentrate and because it helped my nerves. Now I am a non-smoker, it is difficult to believe that those days actually happened. It's like waking up from a nightmare, and that's about the size of it. Nicotine is a drug, and your senses are drugged—your taste buds, your sense of smell. The worst thing about smoking is not the damage to your health or bank account; it's the warping of your mind. You search for any excuse to go on smoking, despite being acutely aware of the harm it is causing.

I remember at one stage switching to a pipe, after another failed attempt to kick cigarettes, in the belief that it was less harmful and would enable me to cut down my intake.

Some of those pipe tobaccos are absolutely foul. The smell can be pleasant, as most pipe tobaccos are infused with artifi-cial aromas, but to start with, they are awful to smoke. I can remember that for about three months the tip of my tongue was as sore as a boil. A liquid mixture of tar collects in the bottom of the bowl of the pipe. Occasionally you unwittingly bring the bowl above the horizontal and before you realize it you have swallowed a mouthful of the filthy stuff. The result is to throw up immediately, no matter whose company you are in.

It took me three months to learn to cope with the pipe, but what I cannot understand is why, during that three months, it didn't occur to me to ask why I was subjecting myself to the torture to begin with.

Of course, once they learn to cope with the pipe, few seem as contented as pipe smokers. Most are convinced that they smoke because they enjoy the pipe. But surely the question is why did they have to work so hard to learn to "enjoy" it when they were perfectly happy without it?

The answer is that once we are hooked, we have to find a way to service our addiction. You need to get this very clear in your mind. You didn't get addicted to nicotine because you fell into the habit of smoking. It's the other way around. You had to get into the habit of smoking to service your addiction.

Even the expression "giving up" is part of the brainwashing. This phrase implies a genuine and substantial sacrifice. The beautiful truth is that there is absolutely nothing to give up. On the contrary, you will be freeing yourself from this terrible slavery and achieving marvelous positive gains. We are going to start to remove this brainwashing now. From this point on, no longer will we refer to "giving up," but to stopping, quitting or the most accurate descriptor of all: ESCAPING!

What tempts us to smoke in the first place is the influence of people already smoking, whether they are the older kids at school, movie stars or our own family. We assume that smokers are getting some tremendous pleasure from smoking and fear that we are missing out on it. We work so hard to become hooked, yet no smoker ever finds out what it is they were missing. Every time we see another smoker we are reassured that there must be something to smoking, otherwise other people wouldn't be doing it.

Because he's brainwashed into believing he has made a genuine sacrifice when he quits, the cigarette continues to dominate the ex-smoker who quits using willpower. This is why people quitting using willpower are often so miserable.

As a child in the 1940s I remember listening to the Paul Temple detective series, which was a very popular program on BBC radio. One episode dealt with marijuana. Some evil-doers were selling cigarettes that contained pot. There were no harmful effects. People merely became addicted and had to go on buying the cigarettes. I was about seven years old when this episode aired. It was the first I had heard of drug addiction and the concept filled me with horror. Even to this day I would not dare take one puff of a joint. How ironic that I should end up addicted to the world's most addictive drug—nicotine. If only Paul Temple had warned me about the tobacco in that cigarette instead of the marijuana! How ironic too that at this time (the immediate post-WWII period) tobacco companies were already aware of the addictiveness of nicotine and were experimenting with ways to increase nicotine yields.

It is incredible to me that we continue to allow tobacco companies to spend billions of dollars persuading healthy teenagers to smoke and that the government itself profits from smokers to the tune of billions of dollars every year.

We are about to remove the brainwashing. It is not the non-smoker who is being deprived but the smoker who is surrendering a lifetime of:

- HEALTH
- ENERGY
- WEALTH
- PEACE OF MIND
- CONFIDENCE
- COURAGE
- SELF-RESPECT
- HAPPINESS
- FREEDOM

And what does he gain from making these enormous sacrifices?

ABSOLUTELY NOTHING! The only thing the cigarette does is remove the aggravation caused by the previous cigarette, so that the smoker, for a moment, feels like a non-smoker.

By lighting up, he temporarily relieves the very slight feeling of emptiness and enjoys the state of relaxation and peace that non-smokers enjoy all their lives. But immediately after putting the cigarette out, the nicotine begins to leave the bloodstream and the slightly empty feeling returns. So the smoker has to light up again, and again and again.

CHAPTER 8

RELIEVING
WITHDRAWAL
PANGS

A s I explained earlier, some smokers claim they smoke for enjoyment, relaxation or some sort of boost. In fact, this is an illusion. The real reason that any smoker lights up is to relieve the withdrawal pangs. Relieving these pangs returns us, for a short while, to a feeling of normality and this is the illusion of pleasure or a boost. The withdrawal pangs themselves are so mild that most smokers are completely unaware that they even exist.

In the very early days we use the cigarette as a social prop. We feel we can take it or leave it. But as the days and weeks go by, the subconscious mind begins to realize that the cigarette appears to relieve the very slight pangs caused by withdrawing from the nicotine contained in the previous cigarette.

Because stress or mild anxiety can feel like the empty, insecure feeling caused by nicotine withdrawal, our subconscious gets tricked into believing that the cigarette will relieve real stress too. Of course we do feel better when we have a cigarette but all we have done is to relieve the stress and discomfort caused by withdrawing from the previous cigarette. At no time has the cigarette helped us to address the real stress or source of anxiety.

As with any drug, our bodies begin to develop immunity to its effects. The more we become hooked on the drug, the greater the need to relieve the withdrawal pangs and the greater the illusion of pleasure or relief. The further we are dragged down, the more we need the artificial boost the cigarette provides. It doesn't take long for us to now consider the state of withdrawal as our natural state, so we need to smoke regularly to feel even a semblance of normality and we become stressed and agitated if we are unable to relieve the withdrawal by smoking. This whole process is so subtle and gradual that most smokers are completely unaware that they are hooked. Instead smokers tell themselves that they have grown to enjoy smoking but cling onto the notion that they could quit anytime they wanted to.

As already stated, smokers tend to relieve their withdrawal pangs at times of stress, boredom, concentration, relaxation or a combination of these. This is explained in greater detail in the next few chapters.

CHAPTER 9

STRESS

I am referring not only to the great tragedies of life, but also to the minor stresses, the socializing, the telephone call, the anxiety of the homemaker with noisy young children and so on.

Let me use the homemaker as an example. This is a very stressful life. Homemakers need to juggle more tasks than even the busiest of businessmen. They need to be part economist, part driver, part cleaner, part cook, part dishwasher, part teacher, part psychologist, part soccer coach…the list is endless. When the smoking homemaker is confronted with an additional stressful situation (for example, the car won't start), her instinct is to want to light a cigarette. She doesn't know why this is, just that it is.

What has actually happened is this. Without being conscious of it, she is already suffering mild aggravation from withdrawing from her previous cigarette. When the additional stress comes, because her subconscious mind associates the relief of stress with cigarettes, she wants to smoke. When she lights up she relieves the stress caused by nicotine withdrawal, and feels better. This boost is not an illusion—she does feel better—but the cigarette has only removed the portion of her stress that was caused by withdrawing from the nicotine in the previous cigarette. Of course, smoking a cigarette has not fixed the car so the real stress still exists. However the smoker now feels better able to cope with the stress because they are temporarily no longer going through the additional stress of withdrawing from nicotine.

This is the illusion of the cigarette as a stress reliever. It temporarily relieves the stress caused by the previous cigarette. But all the smoker is really doing is guaranteeing that he or she will experience withdrawal pangs again and again…

Actually, I believe that even when they are smoking and supposedly relieving stress, smokers are more stressed than non-smokers. There are so few opportunities to smoke nowadays that even when we're smoking we're stressed by the thought of not being able to do so again whenever we wish. Some smokers spend their whole day planning and creating opportunities to smoke. Talk about stress!

I promised you no shock treatment. In the example I am about to give, I am not trying to shock you, I am merely emphasizing that cigarettes create stress rather than relieve it.

Try to imagine getting to the stage where your doctor tells you that unless you stop smoking he is going to have to remove your legs. Just pause for a moment and reflect on that. Try to visualize life without your legs. Try to imagine the frame of mind of a man who, issued with that warning, actually continues to smoke and then has his legs removed.

I used to hear stories like that and dismiss them as cranky. In fact, I used to wish that a doctor would tell me that; then I would have stopped. Yet I was fully expecting any day to have a brain hemorrhage, and lose not only my legs but my life. I didn't think of myself as a crank, just a heavy smoker.

Such stories are not cranky. That is what this awful drug does to you. As you go through life it systematically robs you of your courage and your nerve. The more it ruins your courage, the more you come to rely on the cigarette to restore it. We all know of the panic that smokers experience when they are out late at night and running low on cigarettes. Non-smokers do not experience this fear and panic: the cigarette creates it.

Cigarettes not only destroy your nerves but also contain many toxins that attack the central nervous system and other key organs and systems, progressively destroying your physical health. By the time the smoker reaches the stage at which it is killing him, he depends totally on the cigarette. He sees it as his courage and cannot face life without it.

Get it clear in your mind: Cigarettes don't relieve stress; they create it. Cigarettes don't help you to calm down and relax; they cause you to be panicky and agitated. One of the most wonderful things about breaking free from this awful drug is the return of your courage, confidence and self-esteem.

CHAPTER 10

BOREDOM

If you are already smoking at this moment, you will probably have already forgotten about it until I reminded you.

Another fallacy about smoking is that it relieves boredom. Are smokers who make this claim really saying that cigarettes contain a biologically active ingredient that is a medical cure for boredom? Boredom is a frame of mind, not a medical condition. Anyway, it's not as if the dull, gray fog of boredom is replaced by the brilliant, shining, multi-colored thrill of excitement when a smoker lights up. Initially, you were bored. Now you are bored and smoking.

Just because smokers smoke when they're bored, it doesn't mean that smoking relieves boredom. The fact is that if smoking relieved boredom, smokers would never *be* bored. At the very least they would be significantly less bored than non-smokers, something that is obviously untrue.

What smokers are really saying here is that going for a cigarette provides a momentary distraction if we are bored, in much the same way as any other activity would. The truth is that if you have something to occupy your mind that is not stressful, you can go for long periods without smoking, and it is doesn't bother you in the slightest. It is only when there is no distraction that the smoker will look to smoke. But think about it: if a cigarette relieved boredom, then why would we need to smoke more than one?

As with so much about smoking, the truth is the opposite of the brainwashing we have been subjected to. I believe that smokers have more boredom in their lives than non-smokers because cigarettes rob them of energy and they are more lethargic. Instead of getting up and doing something when they are bored, as a non-smoker does, the smoker tends to want to lounge around, bored, relieving their withdrawal pangs.

Don't take my word for it. See for yourself. Observe smokers who are smoking because they are bored. They still look bored. Anyway, if smokers smoked to relieve boredom, then why do they also smoke when they are not bored?

As an ex-chain-smoker I can assure you that there are no more boring activities in life than lighting up one filthy cigarette after another, day in day out, year in year out.

CHAPTER 11

CONCENTRATION

Cigarettes do not aid concentration. That is yet another illusion.

When you need to concentrate, you automatically try to remove distractions. But the smoker is already distracted: that "little monster" wants his fix, and until he gets is, the smoker will find it difficult to concentrate. So when he wants to concentrate he doesn't even have to think about it. He automatically lights up, removes the distraction caused by needing to smoke and can concentrate properly, like a non-smoker.

Looking at it this way it is obvious that cigarettes do not help concentration, rather that experiencing withdrawal makes it harder to concentrate. Of course non-smokers are not distracted by withdrawal pangs and therefore don't need to smoke to remove them.

There is no question in my mind that cigarettes seriously impair our ability to concentrate. Apart from the constant distraction of going through nicotine withdrawal, the progressive blocking of arteries and veins with the poisons contained in tobacco starves the brain of oxygen.

It was the concentration aspect of smoking that prevented me from succeeding when using the willpower method. I could put up with the irritability and bad temper, but when I really needed to concentrate on something difficult, I *had* to have that cigarette. I can well remember the panic I felt when I discovered that I was not allowed to smoke during my accountancy exams. I was already a chain-smoker and convinced that I would not be able to concentrate for three hours without a cigarette. But I passed the exams, and I can't even remember thinking about smoking at the time, so when it came to the crunch, it obviously didn't bother me.

If we look at the world around us, it's blatantly obvious that cigarettes don't enhance concentration or get our creative juices flowing. If they did then every Nobel Prize winner on the planet would be a smoker, and universities, research institutions and corporations would encourage their staff to smoke. Plato, Homer, Leonardo da Vinci, Michaelangelo and Galileo all seemed to operate at a decent intellectual level without the aid of tobacco.

The loss of concentration that smokers suffer when they try to stop smoking is not, in fact, due to the physical withdrawal from nicotine. When you are a smoker and you have a mental block, what do you do? That's right, if you are not already smoking one, you light a cigarette. That doesn't cure the block, so then what do you do? You do what non-smokers do: you knuckle down and get on with it. Only this time you do so without the distraction of going through nicotine withdrawal. You work through the block—as the non-smoker does—but give the credit to the cigarette. Instead you should be blaming the cigarette for providing the distraction that caused the loss of concentration in the first place. This is a very common theme with respect to smoking. The cigarette gets the credit for everything and the blame for nothing. The moment you stop smoking, everything that goes wrong in your life is blamed on the fact that you've stopped smoking.

Because the willpower quitter has not re-examined this belief, as we have done, he still believes that smoking aids concentration. When he has a mental block, he thinks, "If only I could light up now, it would solve my problem." He then starts to question his decision to quit smoking and this doubt eats away at his resolve—the first step on the road to relapse.

As a footnote to this issue, smokers who claim that the cigarette helps them to concentrate are often the ones who claim that it also relieves boredom. This is interesting because when we're bored we look for distractions and when we want to concentrate we look to remove distractions. So which one is it? Does the cigarette provide a distraction or remove distractions? It obviously can't do both because they are exact opposites, yet because as smokers we unquestioningly accept the brainwashing, we tell ourselves that it can.

When I extinguished my final cigarette, overnight I went from smoking a hundred a day to none, without any loss of concentration.

CHAPTER 12

RELAXATION

Most smokers think that a cigarette helps to relax them. The truth is that nicotine is a chemical stimulant (a poor and inefficient one, but a stimulant nevertheless). Don't take my word for it: take your pulse rate then light a cigarette, take three or four drags in quick succession and check your pulse rate again. You will see a marked increase. How can something that elevates our heart rate and blood pressure be described as "relaxing"?

One of the favorite cigarettes for many smokers is the one after a meal. This is because a meal is a part of the day when we stop working; we sit down and relax and relieve our hunger and thirst. At such times the non-smoker is on a real high, enjoying the opportunity to relax and socialize. However, the poor smoker cannot relax, as he has another hunger he needs to satisfy. He thinks of the cigarette as the icing on the cake, but in reality it is the little monster that needs to be fed, and until he is, the smoker can't relax.

The most uptight, tense people on the planet aren't non-smokers but chain-smokers who are permanently coughing and spluttering, have high blood pressure and are constantly irritable. By this stage cigarettes cease to relieve even partially the symptoms that they have created.

I can remember when I was a young accountant, bringing up a family. One of my children would do something wrong and I would lose my temper to a degree that was out of all proportion to what he had done. I really believed that I had an evil, uncontrollable side to my character. I now know that I did, however it wasn't some inherent flaw in me, but the nicotine "monster" that was rearing its ugly head. During those times I thought I had all the problems in the world, and I wondered what I had done to deserve this miserable, stressful life. Today, I can see the problem so clearly. I was in control of all aspects of my life, bar one. The one thing that controlled me was the cigarette and it was this that was the source of so much unhappiness. The sad thing is that even today I can't convince my children that it was the smoking that caused me to be so irritable.

Some years ago the UK adoption authorities threatened to prevent smokers from adopting children. A man called a radio chat show I was listening to on the subject, irate. He said, "This is completely wrong. I can remember when I was a child, if I had a contentious matter to raise with my mother, I would wait until she lit a cigarette because she was more relaxed then." A smoker views this as proof that cigarettes aid relaxation but the truth is that it just demonstrates that smokers are tense when they *aren't* smoking.

Nicotine withdrawal creates feelings of slight tension and anxiety. When the smoker lights up he removes these feelings and can relax, like a non-smoker. But as soon as he puts the cigarette out, withdrawal begins and the feeling of tension and anxiety returns. So he needs to light up again and again....

This is the saddest thing about smoking. We smoke so that we can remove the feelings of withdrawal and feel like a non-smoker.

Smoking is full of inconsistencies and inaccuracies and one of the biggest is the myth that cigarettes relax us. If they did, smokers would be more relaxed than non-smokers. This is clearly not true. In fact, even most smokers will admit that the opposite is true.

The next time you are in a supermarket and you see a young mother or father screaming at a child, just watch them leave. Nine times out of ten, the first thing they will do is light a cigarette. Start watching smokers, particularly in situations where they are not allowed to smoke. You'll find that they have their hands near their mouths, or they are twiddling their thumbs, or tapping their feet, or fiddling with their hair, or clenching their jaw and grinding their teeth. Smokers aren't relaxed. They've forgotten what it feels like to be completely relaxed. This is one of the many joys you have to look forward to—to once again know what it feels like to be totally relaxed.

The whole business of smoking can be likened to a fly being caught in a pitcher plant. To begin with, the fly is eating the nectar. But at some stage the plant begins to eat the fly. Isn't it time you escaped from the nicotine trap?

CHAPTER 13

COMBINATION CIGARETTES

No, a combination cigarette is not when you are smoking two or more at the same time. When that happens, you begin to wonder why you were smoking the first one. I once burned the back of my hand trying to put a cigarette in my mouth when I already had a lit one there. Actually, it is not quite as stupid as it sounds. As I have already said, eventually the cigarette ceases to relieve the withdrawal pangs, and even when you are smoking, you sense that something is missing. This is the curse of the chain-smoker. Whenever you need a boost, you find that you are already smoking, and this is why so many heavy smokers turn to drink or other drugs. But I digress.

A combination cigarette is one where two or more of our primary triggers for smoking; e.g., boredom, concentration, relaxation and stress are present at the same time. Social functions like parties or weddings are good examples of occasions that can be both stressful and relaxing. This might at first appear to be a contradiction, but it isn't. Any form of socializing can be a little bit stressful, even with friends, and at the same time you are enjoying yourself and relaxing.

There are even situations where all four primary triggers are present at one and the same time. Driving can be one of these. If you are leaving a tense situation, like a visit to the dentist or the doctor, you can now relax. At the same time driving always involves an element of stress. Your life is at stake. You also have to concentrate. And if you are stuck in a traffic jam, or have a long drive on a highway, you may also be bored.

Another classic example is a game of cards. If it's a game like poker, you have to concentrate. If you are losing, it's frustrating which can be stressful. If you have long periods of not getting a decent hand, it can be boring. And, while all this is going on, you are at leisure; you are supposed to be relaxing. During a game of cards, all smokers will be chain-smoking, no matter how slight the withdrawal pangs are. Even so-called "casual" smokers will smoke much more than usual. The ashtrays will fill and overflow in no time. There'll be a constant bluish fog hovering above the table and even the smokers will complain about how smoky the room is getting. If you were to ask any of the smokers whether they were enjoying it, they would look at you as if you were mad. It is often after nights like these, when we wake up with a throat like sandpaper and a mouth like a cesspit that we decide to try to stop smoking.

These combination cigarettes are often considered by smokers to be "special" ones, the ones we think we'll miss the most when we stop smoking. We think that life will never be quite as enjoyable again.

Most of these so-called "special" cigarettes come either at a time that's enjoyable anyway, regardless of whether you are a smoker or a non-smoker (after a meal, a coffee break, having a drink with friends etc.) in which case the cigarette is getting the credit for something that is fun anyway, or after a period of abstinence (after a meal, a coffee break, the first of the day, after a long flight etc.) where we are enjoying not the cigarette, but the ending of the irritation of not being allowed to smoke. This is explained in more detail in the coming chapters.

CHAPTER 14

WHAT AM I
GIVING UP?

ABSOLUTELY NOTHING! The thing that makes it difficult to quit is fear: the fear that we are being deprived
of our pleasure or crutch; the fear that pleasant situations will
never be quite as pleasant without the cigarette; the fear of being
unable to cope with stressful situations.

The effect of the brainwashing is to delude us into believing that we are weak and fragile and that we need something to
help us through the stresses and strains of life. We believe that
stopping smoking will leave a void in our lives.

Get it clear in your mind: CIGARETTES DO NOT FILL
A VOID. THEY CREATE ONE!

These bodies of ours are the most sophisticated machines
on the planet. Whether you believe in a divine creator, a process
of evolution and natural selection or a combination of both,
it is safe to assume that if we were meant to smoke, we would

have been provided with some sort of filter to screen out the hundreds of toxins contained in tobacco smoke.

In fact, our bodies are provided with foolproof systems to enable us to distinguish between food and poison. We don't even need the health warnings on cigarette packs—our body instinctively knows it is being poisoned. When we smoke, our body sends us warning signs in the form of the cough, dizziness, and nausea and we ignore these at our peril.

The beautiful truth is that there is nothing to "give up". Once you purge the "little monster" from your body and the brainwashing from your mind, you will neither want nor need cigarettes.

Cigarettes do not improve meals. They ruin them. They destroy your sense of smell and taste. As a smoker, all you can think about is why everyone else is eating so slowly and when it will end, so that you can smoke. Like I said, it's not so much that we enjoy smoking; it's that we get miserable and anxious when we can't. It doesn't seem to occur to us that non-smokers don't experience this misery and stress.

Because many of us start smoking on social occasions when we are young and a little shy, we acquire the belief that we cannot enjoy social occasions without a cigarette. This is nonsense. Cigarettes systematically attack your nervous system, robbing you of your confidence. The best example of the fear that cigarettes instil in smokers is their effect on women. Many women are fastidious about their personal appearance. They wouldn't dream of going out to a big social function not looking their best and smelling beautiful. Yet knowing that their breath smells like a stale ashtray and their clothes stink appears not to deter them in the least. I know it *bothers* them greatly—many hate the smell of their own hair and clothes— yet it doesn't *deter* them. Such is the fear that this awful drug instills in the smoker.

Cigarettes do not help social occasions; they destroy them. Excusing ourselves every half-an-hour to go and stand outside alone in the freezing cold, smoking half a cigarette, wondering what on earth we are doing and why, stubbing it out in frustration, trying to hide the evidence with a quick spray of breath freshener, going back inside—only to go through the exact same ritual a half hour later. Being constantly self-conscious wondering whether other guests can smell the smoke on you and see the nicotine stains on your teeth and fingers.

Not only is there nothing to give up, there are wonderful positive gains to be had from breaking free from the slavery of smoking. When smokers think about quitting smoking they tend to concentrate on health, money and the social stigma associated with smoking in the twenty-first century. These are obviously valid and important issues, but I personally believe that the greatest gains from stopping are psychological, and they include:

1. The return of your confidence and courage
2. Freedom from the slavery of drug addiction
3. Not having to go through life knowing you are being despised by half of the population and, worst of all, despising yourself

Not only is life better as a non-smoker, it is infinitely more enjoyable. I do not only mean you will be healthier and wealthier. I mean you will be happier and enjoy life far more.

The incredible gains you achieve when you become a non-smoker are discussed in the next few chapters.

Some smokers find it difficult to understand the concept of the "void" I mention, and the following analogy may assist you.

Imagine you have a cold sore on your face. I've got this marvelous ointment. I say to you, "Try this stuff." You rub the ointment on, and the sore disappears immediately. A week later it reappears. You ask, "Do you have any more of that ointment?" I say, "Keep the tube. You might need it again." You apply the ointment. Presto! The sore disappears again. Every time the sore returns, it gets larger and more painful and the period of remission gets shorter and shorter. Eventually the sore covers your whole face and is excruciatingly painful. It is now returning every half hour. You know that the ointment will remove it temporarily, but you are very worried. Will the sore eventually spread over your whole body? Will the periods of remission disappear completely? You go to your doctor. He can't cure it.

By now you are completely dependent on the ointment. You never go out without ensuring that you have a tube with you. If you go abroad you make sure that you take several tubes with you. Now, in addition to the worries about your health, I'm charging you one hundred dollars per tube. You have no choice but to pay me.

Then you read in a newspaper that this isn't just happening to you; many other people have been suffering from the same problem. In fact, researchers have discovered that the ointment doesn't actually cure the sore. All it does is to temporarily push the sore beneath the surface of the skin. Far from curing the cold sore, it is the ointment that has caused it to grow. All you have to do to get rid of the sore is to stop using the ointment. The sore will disappear in due course.

Would you continue to use the ointment?

Would it take you willpower not to use the ointment? If you didn't believe the article you had read in the newspaper, there might be a few days of apprehension, but once you realized that the sore was getting better, the need or desire to use the ointment would go.

Would you be miserable? Of course you wouldn't. You had an awful problem, which you thought was insoluble. Now you've found the solution. Even if it took a while for that sore to disappear completely, each day, as it improved, you'd think, "Isn't is marvelous? I'm not going to die this terrible death."

This was the magic that happened to me when I put out my final cigarette. Let me make one point quite clear in the analogy of the sore and the ointment. The sore isn't lung cancer, arteriosclerosis, emphysema, bronchitis, angina, asthma, or coronary heart disease. These are also caused by the ointment, but in addition to the sore. It isn't the hundreds of thousands of dollars that we burn, or the lifetime of bad breath and stained teeth, the lethargy, the wheezing and coughing. It isn't the lifetime of being despised by a society that seemed happy for you to get hooked in the first place, or the lifetime of despising yourself. These are all in addition to the sore. The sore is the fear that makes us shut our mind to these things, created by that barely noticeable slightly empty, insecure feeling that says, "I want a cigarette." Non-smokers don't suffer from this fear and one of the sweetest things about breaking free from the slavery of smoking is to no longer have your life dominated by fear.

It was as if a great mist had suddenly lifted from my mind. I could see so clearly that the panic feeling of wanting a cigarette wasn't some sort of weakness in me, or some magical quality in the cigarette. Withdrawing from the first cigarette caused that slightly panicky feeling; and each subsequent one, far from relieving the feeling, was keeping it alive. At the same time I could see that all these other "happy" smokers were going through the same nightmare that I was.

For the first time in my smoking life, my fear of quitting was replaced by a feeling of excitement about how wonderful it would be to break free!

CHAPTER 15

SELF-IMPOSED SLAVERY

Usually when smokers try to stop, they quote health, money and the social stigma as their prime motivations. The sheer, unremitting slavery of being a smoker doesn't even occur to us.

We quite rightly view slavery as a great evil, yet every smoker lives the life of a slave, every day they remain a smoker. We seem oblivious to this slavery for the most part, and feel that it is somehow normal. It is far from normal. We were lucky enough to have been born free. Of all the basic human values, surely freedom is the most basic and most important? Who could conceive of anything as stupid as giving away this priceless gift in order to be enslaved to a drug that doesn't even get you high?

Increasingly, smokers are being pushed outside into the cold by society. Anti-smoking by-laws increasingly restrict where and when we can smoke. This bothers smokers, but it doesn't stop them. Ironically, these types of restrictions can make it harder, not easier, to quit. The reason for this is that these days it is impossible to light up whenever you want. As a consequence, smokers go through periods of enforced abstinence throughout the day. As I mentioned, many "special" cigarettes come after a period of abstinence during which the "itch" to smoke has grown and grown. When at last the smoker can scratch the "itch" and light up, the relief is enormous. In effect, these types of smoking restrictions make smokers believe that every cigarette is precious, and that the most important thing on the planet is the next cigarette. However, to a non-smoker it is obvious that the only thing the smoker is getting from the cigarette is temporary relief of the aggravation of needing to smoke.

As an aside, it is interesting to note and also ironic that cigarettes only seem precious to us when we aren't smoking. When we are smoking, we take it for granted and we're barely even aware that we are doing it. It's only when we can't do it that it seems so precious. What a ridiculous state of affairs.

This trend of increased restrictions on smoking is set to continue. Already it is virtually impossible to smoke anywhere in California, and despite the many millions of dollars spent by tobacco companies fighting the establishment of smoking by-laws, thousands of municipalities across the country have implemented or are in the process of implementing similar smoke-free legislation. Gone are the days when you could just light up in a friend's home or a restaurant. Many smokers even have a self-imposed restriction that they won't smoke in their own home. Smokers assimilate these restrictions into their routines out of necessity, but surely the questions we should be asking are: "Why? What is it that the cigarette gives us that is so wonderful that we are prepared to give up our freedom and be treated like a second-class citizen?"

I hated being dominated and controlled in this way. I was in control of every area of my life except for smoking. The cigarette was deciding where I could go, what I could do, when I could do it and with whom.

I remember that during my smoking days, every time I went to church, it was an ordeal. Even during my own daughter's wedding, when I should have been standing there a proud parent, what was I doing? I was thinking, "Let's get on with it, so I can get outside and have a smoke."

I can also remember playing indoor bowls in the winter and pretending to have a weak bladder in order to nip off for a quick smoke. No, this wasn't a fourteen-year-old schoolboy but a forty-year-old chartered accountant. How pathetic. And even when I was back playing the game I wasn't enjoying it. I was looking forward to the finish so that I could smoke again, yet this was supposed to be my way of relaxing and enjoying myself.

I can't even begin to remember how many meals smoking ruined for me. It's funny that we tell ourselves that we enjoy the one after a meal, but the truth is that smoking ruins meals because all you can think about is wolfing down your food as quickly as possible so that you can get back to smoking.

To me one of the tremendous joys of being a non-smoker is to be free from that slavery, to be able to enjoy the whole of my life, not spending half of it not smoking and wishing I could and the other half smoking, wishing I didn't have to. This is a tremendous burden that the smoker carries around with them and it feels wonderful when at last it is lifted from your shoulders.

CHAPTER 16

I'LL SAVE $x EVERY WEEK

I cannot repeat often enough that it is the brainwashing that makes it difficult to stop smoking. Many smokers don't realize this so they need to use variations of the willpower method. The more brainwashing we can remove before you start on your wonderful new life free from the slavery of smoking, the easier and more enjoyable you will find the process.

One of the biggest areas of brainwashing is money. Occasionally I meet someone whom I think of as a confirmed or hardcore smoker. By my definition a confirmed smoker is somebody who can afford it, doesn't believe it injures their health and isn't worried about the social stigma (there are not many about these days).

I do not look for confrontations with smokers—I was one and remember all too well how defensive I would get when the subject of smoking was raised—but they often approach me.

If it's a young man, I say to him, "I can't believe you are not worried about the money."

Usually, his eyes light up. If I had attacked him on health grounds or on the social stigma, he would feel at a disadvantage, but on money—"Oh, I can afford it. It is only $x a week and I think it's worth it. It is my only vice or pleasure."

If he is a pack-a-day smoker I say to him, "I still cannot believe you are not worried about the money. You will need to earn over $150,000 in your lifetime to finance your addiction. What are you doing with that money? You are not even setting light to it or throwing it away. You are actually using that money to ruin your physical health, to destroy your courage and confidence, and to suffer a lifetime of slavery, bad breath and stained teeth. These are all priceless and irreplaceable. It's like paying an assassin to kill you. Surely that must worry you?"

It becomes apparent at this point, particularly with younger smokers, that it is the first time they have ever considered smoking as a lifetime expense. For most smokers the price of a pack is bad enough. Occasionally we work out what we spend in a week, and that is alarming. Very occasionally (and only when we're thinking about stopping) we estimate what we spend in a year and that is frightening, but over a lifetime—it's unthinkable.

The confirmed smoker with whom I am having the discussion almost always counters with the encyclopedia salesman trick. "I can afford it. It is only so much a week." I know this trick well, having used it myself for years. I then say, "I will make you an offer you cannot refuse. You pay me the cost of one year of smoking right now and I will provide you with free cigarettes for the rest of your life."

If I were offering to take over his $150,000 mortgage for $2,000, the smoker would have my signature on a contract faster than you could say "Philip Morris," and yet not one confirmed smoker (and please bear in mind I am not talking to someone like yourself who plans to stop, I am talking to someone who claims to have no intention of stopping) has taken me up on that offer. Why not? Is it because, deep down, like every other smoker on the planet, even "confirmed" smokers would really rather be non-smokers?

Often at this point in my consultations, a smoker will say, "Look, I am not really worried about the money aspect." If you are thinking along these lines, ask yourself why you are not worried. In other areas of our lives we go to great trouble to save a couple of dollars. We clip coupons. We wait until our favorite stores have a sale. We make sure we claim every last cent on our taxes. Yet here we are spending tens, if not hundreds of thousands of dollars for the privilege of poisoning ourselves to death.

The answer to the question is this. Every other decision that you make in your life will be the result of an analytical process of weighing the pros and cons of various courses of action and arriving at a rational, fact-based decision. From time to time we may get it wrong, but at least the process will be a rational one. Whenever any smoker weighs up the pros and cons of smoking, the answer is the same: "STOP SMOKING! YOU FOOL!" We can do this exercise a thousand times and a thousand times the answer would be the same. We have two options at this stage: to sacrifice the cigarette, or sacrifice rationality. So we sacrifice rationality. We sense that we are not smoking because we want to or because we like it, but because we think we can't stop. We have to keep our head in the sand and believe the brainwashing, because otherwise we feel stupid being a smoker.

Try to take your head out of the sand for a moment. Smoking is a chain reaction. Withdrawing from your first cigarette made you smoke the second. Withdrawing from the second made you smoke the third and so on. Actually, the first cigarette you ever smoked cost you everything you have ever spent on cigarettes. That was one very expensive cigarette! Equally, your next cigarette will cost you everything you will ever spend in the future on cigarettes. If you do not break the chain, you will be a smoker for the rest of your life. Now estimate how much you would spend on smoking for the rest of your life. The amount will vary from individual to individual, but for the purposes of this exercise let us assume it is $50,000.

You will shortly be making the decision to smoke your final cigarette (not yet, please—remember the initial instructions). All you have to do to remain a happy non-smoker is not to fall for the trap again. That is, do not smoke that first cigarette. If you do, that one cigarette will cost you $50,000.

If you think that this is a trick way of looking at it, don't kid yourself. Just work out how much money you would have saved if you hadn't smoked your first cigarette.

Actually, this is the only sensible and accurate way to look at the true financial cost of smoking. Just think how you would feel if a check for $50,000 from a competition you'd won were to arrive in the mail. You'd be dancing with delight! So start dancing, because with the decision you have made to escape from the smoking trap, you have just saved yourself $50,000.

This is a great deal of money, and you should quite rightly celebrate this windfall, but the truth is that a substantially improved financial status is the smallest and least important of the gains you earn when you break free from smoking. You are also giving yourself the gifts of life and freedom. These are truly priceless, and they just aren't available to smokers.

During the withdrawal period you may be tempted to have "just one more" final cigarette. Of course that "one more" will lead to another and another and soon enough, you'll be back smoking as you are now. It will help if you remind yourself it will cost you $50,000 (or whatever your estimate is). Would you spend $50,000 to get re-addicted to a drug that doesn't even get you high?

If you are ever in the company of "happy" smokers who tell you how much they enjoy it, just tell them that you know an idiot called Allen Carr who, if you pay him a year's smoking money in advance, will provide free cigarettes for the rest of your life. Perhaps you can find me someone who will take up the offer?

CHAPTER 17

HEALTH

This is the area where the brainwashing is at its peak. Smokers think they are aware of the health risks. They are not.

Even in my case, when I was expecting my head to explode at any moment and honestly believed I was prepared to accept the consequences, I was still kidding myself.

If in those days I had taken a cigarette out of the pack and an alarm started to sound, followed by a voice saying, "OK Allen, this is the one! Fortunately you get a warning and this is it. If you smoke another cigarette your head will explode," do you think I would have lit that cigarette?

There is absolutely no doubt in my mind that I would *not* have lit that cigarette. In addition, I would have been immensely relieved to have received the warning and happy that my head was not going to explode.

I did what every smoker on the planet does throughout their smoking lives: I closed my mind, prayed it wouldn't be me, kept my head firmly in the sand and hoped that I would wake up one morning with no desire to smoke. Smokers can't allow themselves to think about the health risks because if they do, even the illusion of enjoyment disappears.

This explains why the shock tactics used by the media on the Great American Smokeout are so ineffective. It is only non-smokers who can bring themselves to watch these horrific ads. It also explains why smokers, recalling Uncle Fred who smoked forty a day until he was eighty, will ignore the millions of smokers who are cut down in their prime because of this poisonous weed.

I frequently have the following conversation with smokers (usually the younger ones):

ME: Why do you want to stop?

SMOKER: I can't afford it.

ME: Aren't you worried about the health risks?

SMOKER: No. I could step under a bus tomorrow.

ME: Would you deliberately step under a bus?

SMOKER: Of course not.

ME: Do you bother to look both ways when you cross the road?

SMOKER: Of course I do.

Exactly. The smoker goes to a lot of trouble not to step under a bus, and the odds are hundreds of thousands to one against it happening. Yet the smoker risks the near certainty of being crippled by smoking and seems oblivious to the risks. Such is the power of the brainwashing.

I remember one famous British golfer who wouldn't travel to the US to play because he was afraid of flying. Yet he would chain-smoke round the golf course. Isn't it strange that if we felt there was the slightest fault in an aircraft, we wouldn't go up in it, yet we accept the one-in-two odds that smoking will kill or disable us? And what is our reward for taking this truly staggering risk? ABSOLUTELY NOTHING.

Smoking is easily the biggest cause of preventable death in the world. It is estimated that every year around five million deaths are caused by smoking (including over 450,000 in the US). Sometimes it can be difficult to even begin to get our head around something on that scale. To give you a comparison, this is like having a September 11th every four hours, twenty-four hours a day, 365 days a year.

Another common myth about smoking is the "smoker's cough." Many of the younger people who attend our seminars are not worried about their health because they do not have a smoker's cough. Some say that smokers who *don't* have a cough are the ones who should worry the most. A cough is one of nature's fail-safe methods for expelling foreign matter and poisons from the lungs. The cough itself is not a disease; it is a symptom. When smokers cough it is because their lungs are trying to get rid of the cancer-triggering tars and irritants contained in tobacco smoke. When they don't cough, the poison remains in their lungs, and this is when they can cause cancer and the many other horrendous diseases associated with smoking. Smokers tend to avoid exercise and get into the habit of shallow breathing in order not to cough. I used to believe that my smoker's cough was going to kill me. In truth, by expelling much of the filth from my lungs, it probably added years to my life.

Just think of it this way. If you had a nice new car and allowed it to rust without bothering to do anything about it, that would be pretty stupid. It wouldn't be the end of the world though; it is only a question of money and you could always buy another. Your body is the vehicle that carries you through life. You only get one. It's a cliché that our health is our most valued asset. How true that is, as any sick millionaire will tell you. Who could conceive of a more ridiculous pastime than to spend a fortune for the privilege of poisoning the vehicle upon which your very life depends?

Wise up. You don't have to smoke, and remember: it is doing ABSOLUTELY NOTHING FOR YOU.

Just for a moment take your head out of the sand and ask yourself, if you knew for certain that your next cigarette would be the one that triggered off the cancer in your body, whether you would actually smoke it. Forget the disease itself (it's difficult to imagine something so painful) but imagine that you have to go to your local cancer hospital to suffer through the endless rounds of chemo. Now you are not planning the rest of your life. You are planning your death. What is going to happen to your family and loved ones? How would it feel to have your hopes and dreams smashed to a pulp in a single heartbeat? Your whole life snatched from you to be replaced by emptiness, terror and an excruciatingly painful and humiliating death? How would you even begin to explain it to your children?

The saddest part of my job is that I often see people to whom this has happened. Of course, they are just like you and me, they never thought it would happen to them either, but it does. The worst thing that happens isn't even the disease itself; it's the knowledge that they only have themselves to blame and the guilt they feel towards their innocent families. All our lives as smokers we say, "I'll quit tomorrow." But tomorrow never comes, does it?

Those poor smokers all say the same thing: "If only I could turn the clock back." Sadly, this is the one thing they can't do.

You have a golden opportunity to save your life by breaking free from this awful addiction and the limitless pain and suffering it brings to so many millions of lives. You have a choice. Make no mistake; if you choose to continue to smoke after reading this book, you'll be a smoker for the rest of your life. Is this really the future you are choosing for yourself and your family?

At the beginning of the book I promised you no scare tactics. If you have already decided to become a non-smoker, this does not fall into that category. If you are still in doubt, skip the remainder of this chapter and come back to it when you have read the rest of the book.

Volumes of statistics have already been published about the damage that cigarettes can cause to the smoker's health. The trouble is that until the smoker decides it is time to stop, he goes to great lengths to avoid being exposed to such information. He doesn't want to know. Even the on-pack health warning is a waste of time because the smoker doesn't even register it. And if he does see the warning, it is likely to cause anxiety and stress, which will make him want a cigarette.

Smokers tend to think of the health hazard as a hit-or-miss affair, a bit like Russian roulette. Get it into your head: the deterioration to your health is already happening. Every time you take a drag you are breathing cancer-triggering fumes deep into your lungs, and lung cancer—horrific as it is—is by no means the worst of the killer diseases that cigarettes cause or contribute to.

While I was still smoking, I'd never heard of arteriosclerosis or emphysema. I knew the permanent wheezing and coughing and the increasingly frequent attacks of bronchitis and asthma were a direct result of my smoking. But although they caused me real discomfort there was no real pain.

I confess that the thought of contracting lung cancer terrified me, which is probably why I just blocked it from my mind. It's amazing how the fear of the horrendous health risks associated with smoking is overshadowed by the fear of stopping. It's not so much that the fear of quitting is greater; just that it's a more immediate one. The fear of contracting lung cancer is a fear of something that might happen at some point in the future, so we can distance ourselves from the risk and the fear it creates. We think, "Who knows? I might not get it. Surely I will have quit by then?"

We tend to think of smoking as a tug-of-war. On the one side we have the fear that it's killing us, costing a fortune and making us a slave and an addict. On the other side, it's our pleasure or crutch. It never occurs to us that these perceived "benefits" of smoking are really just more thinly disguised fears: the fear that I won't be able to have fun, relax or handle stress without the cigarette. Of course both sets of fear are caused by the cigarette. And I hardly need to point out that non-smokers have none of these fears.

As I have said before, it's not so much that we genuinely enjoy smoking, but that we get miserable when we can't. This is not genuine pleasure, it is an attempt to avoid discomfort—a discomfort that non-smokers don't get.

Think of a heroin addict deprived of his drug and going through withdrawal. He is miserable, stressed, panicky and experiencing severe physical symptoms. Now picture that same addict's utter relief when he shoots up and is able to remove those awful symptoms. Non-heroin addicts don't suffer that panic feeling. The heroin causes it. The subsequent dose partially relieves the symptoms, but also ensures that addict will go through withdrawal again. So the addict shoots up again to remove the symptoms and the cycle of addiction continues. Why is all this so obvious with other people's addictions, but not our own?

Non-smokers don't get anxious, panicky or stressed when they can't smoke. The cigarette causes those symptoms and the next cigarette partially relieves them. But the smoker withdraws from that cigarette too, and the need to smoke returns. So the smoker has to light up again and again.

The fear of contracting lung cancer scared me but didn't make me quit because I believed it was rather like walking through a minefield. You either got away with it or you didn't. It didn't even occur to me that I didn't have to walk through the minefield in the first place. I felt that I knew the risks and that it was my own business and nobody else's. If a non-smoker ever tried to make me aware of those risks I would defend my rights vigorously, using the evasive tactics all addicts adopt to attempt to justify the unjustifiable.

"You have to die of something."
Of course you do, but is that a logical reason for deliberately shortening your life?

"Quality of life is more important than longevity."
Exactly, but surely you are not suggesting that the quality of life of an alcoholic or heroin addict is better than that of someone that isn't addicted to alcohol or heroin? Do you really believe that a smoker's quality of life is better than a non-smoker's? Surely the smoker loses on both counts—his life is both shorter and more miserable.

"My lungs probably suffer more damage from car exhaust fumes than from smoking."
Even if that were true (it isn't), is that a logical reason for punishing your lungs further? Can you possibly conceive of anyone being stupid enough to actually put their mouth over a tailpipe and deliberately inhale those fumes into their lungs? And pay for the privilege?

THAT'S WHAT SMOKERS EFFECTIVELY DO!
Think of that next time you watch a smoker inhale good and deep on one of those "precious" cigarettes!

I can understand why the congestion and the risks of contracting lung cancer didn't help me quit. I could cope with the former and close my mind to the latter. As you are already aware, my method is not to frighten you into quitting, but the complete opposite—to make you realize just how more enjoyable your life will be when you have escaped.

However, I do believe that if I could have seen what was happening inside my body, this would have helped me to quit. Now I'm not referring to the shock technique of showing the smoker's lung next to that of a non-smoker (I figured that both subjects were pretty dead). Anyway, it was obvious to me from my nicotine stained teeth and fingers that my lungs were unlikely to be a pretty sight. Provided they kept functioning, they were less of an embarrassment than my teeth, breath and fingers—at least no-one could see or smell my lungs.

What I am referring to is the progressive clogging up of our arteries and veins and the gradual deterioration of every muscle and organ caused by depriving them of oxygen and other nutrients. Even worse is that we replace these nutrients with poison and deadly compounds such as carbon monoxide.

Like the majority of motorists, I don't like the thought of dirty oil or a dirty oil filter in my car engine. Could you imagine buying a brand new Cadillac and never changing the oil or the oil filter? Or even worse, deliberately adding impurities that you know will ruin the engine? That is precisely what we do to our bodies when we become smokers.

Until very recently, the tobacco industry denied that nicotine is addictive (to this day the word "addictive" does not appear on US cigarette pack health warnings) or that smoking causes lung cancer, heart disease, emphysema etc. The industry and its apologists hide behind an argument based on something called etiology. Their argument goes something like this: because we know that many things (possibly thousands) might contribute to the formation of cancer cells, it is impossible to blame one thing (i.e. the cigarette), so long as even one of these other so-called confounding factors is also present. You can never be certain, they argue, which caused the cancer. Using this as a model, it is impossible to prove that banging your head against a brick wall causes headaches, so long as another co-factor (listening to Swiss yodeling music, for example) is present.

While I strongly support the right of everyone to have their own opinion, they are not entitled to their own facts. To argue that smoking doesn't cause these diseases is stupid and dangerous. I also find it incredibly callous and disrespectful to the millions of smokers who have paid the ultimate price, to say nothing of their families left behind.

One needs only to see the mountain of cigarette butts outside the cancer wards of hospitals around the country to see the link between the two.

The statistical evidence in support of the dangers of smoking is so overwhelming as not to need further debate here. No one ever scientifically proved to me exactly why, when I bang my thumb with a hammer, it hurts. I soon got the message.

I must emphasize that I am not a doctor, but I didn't need to be to know that my permanent cough, congestion, frequent asthma and bronchitis attacks were directly related to my smoking. This was confirmed to me in the strongest possible way when I quit smoking and all of the symptoms either disappeared or improved dramatically. You don't need to be a doctor—or a rocket scientist—to know that smoking is bad for you. The only question in the smoker's mind is whether they can survive it or whether it'll kill them.

In my view, the most devastating damage the smoker experiences is to his immune system. Every species on the planet is under constant attack from germs, viruses, parasites, etc. The best defense we have is our immune system, which routinely protects us from these types of attacks. But how can our immune system function effectively when we are starving our body of the oxygen and nutrients it needs to thrive and survive? How can it work properly for you when it is under constant attack from the poisons contained in tobacco smoke? It's bad enough that smoking causes so many life-threatening conditions, but what is worse is that it on top of this, it also works, like AIDS, to brutalize our immune system making us less able to fight off other diseases, infections and conditions.

Many of the adverse effects that smoking had on my health, some of which I had been suffering from for years, did not become apparent to me until many years after I had quit smoking.

While I was busy despising those idiots and cranks who would rather lose their legs than quit smoking, it didn't even occur to me that I was already suffering from arteriosclerosis myself. I attributed my gray complexion to my natural coloring and an unhealthy aversion to exercise. I didn't realize that it was due to the blocking up of my capillaries caused by smoking (incidentally along with smelling a lot nicer, a vastly improved complexion is one of the first things that people will notice about you when you quit, and it usually happens within a week or so). I had varicose veins in my thirties, which have disappeared since I stopped. About five years before I quit I began to have this weird sensation in my legs. It wasn't a sharp pain, just a persistent, restless, slightly sore stiffness. I would get Joyce to massage my legs every night. About a year after I quit I realized that I hadn't needed a massage since a few days after quitting.

About two years before I quit, I would occasionally get violent pains in my chest, which I feared must be lung cancer but now assume to have been angina. I haven't had a single attack since I quit.

When I was a child I used to bleed profusely from cuts. This frightened me. No one explained to me that bleeding was a natural and necessary part of the healing process and that the blood would clot when it needed to. Later in life I would sustain quite deep cuts yet hardly bleed at all. This brown-red gunge would ooze from the cut.

The color worried me. I knew that blood was meant to be bright red and I assumed I had some sort of blood disease. However I was pleased about the consistency, because it meant I no longer bled so profusely. Not until I quit did I learn that smoking thickens the consistency of your blood and that the brownish color was due to the lack of oxygen. It didn't particularly bother me at the time because I was blissfully ignorant, but today with hindsight it is this that scares me the most about smoking. I used to deny that smoking caused heart disease. In fact, it's a miracle our hearts can stand up to the punishment—being required to pump this ever-thickening gunge throughout our body without ever once missing a beat. It made me realize, not how fragile we are, but how robust, strong and ingenious that incredible machine is!

I had liver spots on my hands by the age of forty. In case you don't know, liver spots are those rather unsightly brown or white spots that some older people have on their face and hands. I tried to ignore them. Five years after I quit I was conducting a seminar when an attendee mentioned that when he had quit previously, his liver spots had disappeared. I had completely forgotten about mine and, to my amazement, they too had disappeared.

For as long as I could remember I would see stars if I sneezed, or stood up too quickly. If I was in a hot bath and stood up I would get dizzy, as if I was about to black out. I never related this to smoking. In fact I was convinced that everyone felt this way and that I was normal. About ten years ago an ex-smoker told me about this and it dawned on me that I no longer experienced any of these conditions related to circulation. When I was a smoker I could never get my fingers or toes warm in winter. No matter how long I spent indoors by the fire, my extremities would remain stone cold. I quit in July 1983, and have never been cold since, as my circulation bounced back remarkably after thirty-three years of abuse.

You might conclude that I am somewhat of a hypochondriac. I think I probably was when I was a smoker. One of the great scams of smoking is that we are led to believe that the cigarette gives us courage when in fact it leaves your courage, your nerve and your self-confidence shot to pieces. I was shocked when I heard my father say that he had no wish to live to be fifty. Little did I realize twenty years later I'd be saying the same. I had completely lost my *joie de vivre*. You might conclude that this chapter has been one of necessary (or unnecessary) doom and gloom. I promise you that it is the exact opposite.

When I was a child I used to fear death. I used to think that smoking removed that fear (I know now that it doesn't, just that as a smoker you have to learn to ignore it). Smoking also gave me a new fear though: A FEAR OF LIVING!

Now my fear of dying has returned. It doesn't bother me. I realize that it only exists because I have rediscovered my love of life. I don't brood over my fear of dying any more than I did when I was a child. I'm far too busy having fun and living life to the full to dwell on it. The odds of me living until I'm a hundred are slim to none, but I'll try, and I'll enjoy every precious moment.

There were two other advantages on the health side that never occurred to me until I had stopped smoking. One was that I used to have persistent nightmares that I was being chased. I can only assume that this was triggered by the slightly empty, insecure feeling of withdrawal and then exaggerated by my sub-conscious. Now the only nightmare I ever have is that very occasionally I dream that I am smoking. This is quite a common dream among ex-smokers. Some worry that it shows a deep seated sub-conscious desire to smoke, but I think the fact that it's a nightmare shows that you are happy not to have to smoke any more.

When I described being "chased" every night in a dream, I originally mistakenly typed "chaste." Perhaps this was just a Freudian slip, but it does lead me conveniently into the second advantage. At my seminars, when discussing the effect that smoking has on concentration, I will sometimes ask: "Which organ in the body has the greatest need of a good supply of blood?" The stupid grins, usually on the faces of the men in the group, would indicate that they had missed the point. However, they were absolutely right. Being a somewhat reserved Englishman, I find the subject of sex rather embarrassing, and I have no intention of doing a miniature Kinsey report by detailing the adverse effect that smoking had on my own sex life, or on those of other ex-smokers with whom I have discussed the subject. Again, I was not aware of the impact of smoking on sex drive and performance. I had attributed my sexual prowess and activity, or rather lack of it, to advancing years.

However, if you watch natural history programs, as I do, you will be aware that the first "rule" of nature is survival and that the second is reproduction. Nature ensures that reproduction does not take place unless both partners are physically healthy and able to provide food, shelter and protection for the offspring. Man's ingenuity has enabled him to bend these rules somewhat; however I know for a fact that smoking causes impotence. I can also assure you that when you feel fit and healthy, you'll enjoy sex much more and more often.

The purpose of this chapter has not been to scare you into wanting to quit smoking. If scare tactics were going to work, they would have done so a long time ago. What I have attempted to do is to demonstrate that the brainwashing closes our minds to the true physical cost of smoking, and that life is so much more enjoyable without carrying this tremendous burden of fear around with you.

The effect of the brainwashing is that we tend to think like the man who, having fallen off a one hundred-story building is heard to say as he passes the fiftieth floor, "So far so good!" We think that as we have got away with it up until now, one more cigarette won't make the difference.

Try to see it another way: the "habit" is a lifetime's chain of fear, disease, misery and slavery, each cigarette creating the need for the next. When you start smoking you light a fuse. The trouble is, YOU DON'T KNOW HOW LONG THE FUSE IS. Every time you light a cigarette you are one step nearer to the bomb exploding. HOW WILL YOU KNOW IF IT'S THE NEXT ONE?

CHAPTER 18

ENERGY

Most smokers are aware of the effect that the process of clogging up and depriving the body of oxygen and nutrients has on their general health. However, they are not so aware of the effect it has on their energy levels.

One of the subtleties of the smoking trap is that the effects it has on us, both mental and physical, happen so gradually that the changes are almost imperceptible to us, and we consider them to be the normal signs of getting older.

It is very similar to the effects of poor eating habits. The potbelly appears so gradually that it causes us no alarm.

But suppose it happened overnight. You went to bed trim, not an ounce of fat and a six-pack stomach. You awoke the following morning, thirty pounds heavier, with no muscle definition and a gut that puts your plans to go to the beach on hold indefinitely. Instead of waking up feeling fully rested and full of energy, you feel miserable and lethargic. If that happened you would be panic-stricken, wondering what awful disease you had contracted overnight. Yet the disease is the same. The fact it took twenty years to get there is irrelevant.

So it is with smoking. If I had a time machine that could transport you forward in time just three weeks to experience the mental and physical benefits of quitting, that is all I'd need to do to persuade you to quit. You would think: "Will I really look and feel that good?" Actually, what it really amounts to is, "Have I really sunk this low?" I emphasize that the benefits are not only physical; you will have tons more energy, confidence, courage and self-esteem. You'll also be more able to relax, concentrate and handle stress.

As a teenager I remember rushing around just for the hell of it. I had so much energy. It was fantastic! Then for thirty-three years I was permanently tired and lethargic. I used to struggle to drag myself out of bed in the morning, and after my evening meal it was all I could do to lie on the sofa in front of the TV. I'd be asleep within minutes. Because my father used to be the same, I thought this behavior was normal. I thought that only young kids and teenagers had energy, and that middle age started in your early twenties.

Shortly after putting out my final cigarette, the congestion that I had felt in my lungs for years disappeared along with my smoker's cough. My attacks of bronchitis and asthma stopped overnight, never to return. However something even better also happened—all the more delightful because it was so unexpected. I started waking up at seven in the morning feeling completely rested and full of energy actually wanting to exercise, jog and swim. At forty-eight I couldn't run a step or swim a stroke. My sporting activities were confined to such intensely athletic pursuits as lawn bowling and golf, for which I had to use a cart. Today, at age seventy-two I jog two to three miles a day, work out for thirty minutes in the gym and swim twenty lengths. It's great to have energy, and when you feel mentally and physically strong, it feels great to be alive.

Unfortunately I don't have a time machine, so I can't show you how you will look and feel in three week's time. However, you will instinctively know that what I'm saying is true. Grasp this wonderful opportunity and enjoy the benefits of breaking free from this unremitting, unrewarding addiction. Begin to let yourself get excited about this wonderful thing you are doing for yourself. USE YOUR IMAGINATION!

CHAPTER 19

IT RELAXES ME AND GIVES ME CONFIDENCE

This is the very worst fallacy of all about smoking, and for me it ranks alongside the ending of the slavery as being the greatest benefit to quitting—not to have to go through your whole life with the permanent feeling of insecurity that smokers suffer from.

Some smokers find it difficult to believe that the cigarette actually causes that insecure, slightly panicky feeling you get when you are out late at night and realize that you're running low on cigarettes. This is because we have been brainwashed into believing that smoking relieves this feeling. But non-smokers don't ever have that feeling, so the only conclusion we can come to is that the cigarette creates it. We fall for a con trick: we acknowledge the slight boost that the cigarette gives us by partially removing the slight feeling of emptiness and insecurity when we light up, but we conveniently forget that it was withdrawing from the previous cigarette that created those symptoms in the first place.

As a smoker the only thing we look forward to is the next opportunity to smoke, and we go out of our way to create such opportunities. This burden creates even more stress for the smoker on top of the existing stress of going through permanent nicotine withdrawal and the stress of bombarding your body with hundreds of toxic chemicals twenty times a day.

It's blatantly obvious to non-smokers that smoking is one of the *more stressful* and *least* relaxing pursuits. Even when smokers are smoking they aren't relaxed, unless they're in a situation where they can light up whenever they wish. This perhaps explains why so many smokers have problems with alcohol; they are forced to spend time in places where they are able to smoke. This attracts smokers to bars, one of the few places it is still possible (in some places) to smoke. You only need to see the smoke-filled rooms of AA meetings to appreciate the link between tobacco and alcohol. This also explains the smoker's love of casinos and bingo halls!

It is truly ironic that we look to the cigarette to relax us when in fact it creates the stress in the first place. Smoking for relaxation is like drinking bourbon to get sober.

When I finally broke free from the smoking trap I was astonished to realize that I was far more relaxed and confident as a non-smoker. Such is the brainwashing that I thought that I would never be able to relax without a cigarette. The truth is that as a smoker, I didn't know how it felt to really relax because I was in a permanent state of stress caused by smoking. And I was certain that cigarettes gave me confidence. I now realize that this was also an illusion. Because I got panicky when I couldn't smoke, I assumed that the cigarette gave me courage and confidence. It never occurred to me that non-smokers don't have that panic feeling and they therefore don't need the artificial boost (of removing the symptoms of withdrawal created by the previous cigarette) the cigarette gives.

In the last years of my smoking, I was a nervous wreck. I refused to have a medical checkup, because I was terrified of what it would reveal. If I wanted to buy life insurance or private health coverage I insisted on a "no medical" product and paid far higher premiums as a result. I hated visiting hospitals, doctors and dentists. I also had a terrible fear of the future and of aging—as a smoker, I didn't feel I was entitled to a future.

I didn't relate any of this to my smoking, but when I stopped I suddenly acquired the confidence and courage to face these issues head on. Nowadays I look forward to every day. Of course, bad things happen in my life—this is the human condition—and I am subject to the normal stress and strains, but it is wonderful to have the confidence and courage to deal with them. And the improved health, energy and freedom make the good times more enjoyable too.

CHAPTER 20

THOSE SINISTER BLACK SHADOWS

Another of the great joys of breaking free from the slavery of smoking is to be free from those sinister black shadows that lurk at the back of every smoker's mind. All smokers sense they have been trapped, and to make a bad situation tolerable, we have to close our minds to the ill-effects of smoking. For most of our lives smoking is virtually automatic, but those black shadows are always lurking in our sub-conscious minds, never very far beneath the surface.

There are many substantial advantages to becoming a happy non-smoker. Some of them are pretty obvious—vastly improved health, a much-improved financial status and ending to the slavery of smoking—but such was my fear of life without cigarettes that I was prepared to ignore these obvious advantages and search desperately for any flimsy excuse to keep smoking.

We can get very creative when looking for an excuse to smoke and I was at my most creative when I was actually supposed to be trying to quit. This creativity was triggered by the desperation that came from the fear and misery I felt by having to use willpower.

Smokers can't block their minds to the health and financial aspects of smoking—they are just too big and too obvious to ignore—but I still struggle to understand how I could have blocked my mind to the sheer slavery of smoking. Spending half of my life not smoking, wishing I could, and the other half smoking, wishing I didn't have to.

In the last chapter I mentioned the incredible joy I experienced when I rediscovered my energy and confidence but this pales into insignificance next to the joy I felt when at last those sinister black clouds that for years had been hanging over me, disappeared forever, leaving me for the first time in my adult life a truly free man.

Smokers are not the weak-willed, spineless jellyfish that anti-smokers (and even some smokers themselves) believe.

I knew that I was strong-willed and I was in control of every other aspect of my life. I loathed myself for being dependent on something I despised so much and that I knew was ruining my life and my family's future.

I cannot even begin to describe to you the utter joy of being free from these sinister black shadows, the dependency and the self-loathing. I can't tell you how nice it is to be able to look at smokers not with a feeling of envy, but with a feeling of pity for them and a sense of elation that you have broken free and are no longer trapped.

The last two chapters have dealt with the considerable advantages of being a non-smoker. In the interests of fair play and with a desire to give a balanced account, the next chapter lists the advantages of being a smoker.

CHAPTER 21

THE ADVANTAGES OF BEING A SMOKER

CHAPTER 22

THE WILLPOWER METHOD OF STOPPING

It is an accepted "fact" in our society that it is very difficult to stop smoking. Even books advising you how to quit usually start off by telling you how difficult and unpleasant the whole process is. The truth is that if you go about it the right way (i.e., follow the instructions in this book) it is ridiculously easy. I can understand why people might question that statement, but just consider it in detail for a moment.

If your aim is to run a four-minute mile, that's difficult. You will have to undergo years of extremely hard training, and even then you may be physically incapable of doing it. In fact, until Roger Bannister broke the four-minute barrier, it was considered impossible.

As a smoker about to attempt to quit, you might feel that you're about to attempt the impossible, but really all you need do is not light your next cigarette. After all, no one forces you to smoke. Unlike food or drink, cigarettes are not necessary for survival. So if you want to stop, why would it be difficult? In fact, it isn't. It is smokers who make it difficult by relying on the willpower method. I define the willpower method as any method that makes the smoker feel that he or she is making a sacrifice. Let's look at this in more detail.

You never decided that you would become a smoker for life. You experimented with a few cigarettes and because they tasted so awful, you believed that you could never get hooked and were convinced that you could stop whenever you wished.

Before we realize it, we're buying them and we begin to feel uneasy if we don't have cigarettes close at hand or if we are going into a situation where we won't be able to smoke. Smoking, very quietly but very definitely, has become part of our lives. We always have our cigarettes close at hand and we begin to believe that they help us relax, concentrate, handle stress, etc. We come to rely on the cigarette to give us a "boost" in a wide variety of situations. We conveniently ignore the many contradictions that surround smoking. Like the fact that we use a cigarette as a stimulant in the morning to help us get going, and as a relaxant in the evening to help us "take the edge off." It also doesn't occur to us that non-smokers seem to get on perfectly well without them. Whether we openly admit it or not, soon we are smoking because we don't think we can stop.

Research has shown that nicotine addiction takes place very quickly, but because it is so subtle (unlike, say, heroin addiction where the effects of the drug are plain to see) it can take smokers years to realize that they are hooked. This is because we are brainwashed into believing that we smoke because we enjoy it. This is distorted thinking: because we get miserable when we can't smoke, we assume it gives us great pleasure when we do.

Usually it is only when we try to stop for the first time that we realize we have a problem. The first attempts to stop are more often than not in the early days and are triggered by a shortage of cash as a student or by a realization that we are short of breath playing sports.

These "trigger" events are stressful in themselves, and ironically, it is during times of stress when our need to smoke is its greatest. We are therefore attempting what we perceive to be an extremely stressful undertaking (quitting smoking) at a time when we are already stressed and "need" to smoke most. We quickly conclude that doing without our "crutch" at a time of such stress is not an option (it never occurs to us that the cigarette is causing some of the stress), so we begin to look for an excuse to smoke. We tell ourselves that it "wasn't the right time" to quit. So we decide to wait until there is less stress or no stress in our lives before trying again. Of course, this gives us the perfect excuse to keep smoking indefinitely because so long as you are smoking, you will have stress. If we ever do have a period when we aren't stressed we don't quit because we need the stress to provide the motivation to do so.

This becomes a common pattern among what we call "serial quitters." On the one hand we sense that being a smoker is stressful, but during our whole lives we have been brainwashed into believing that cigarettes relieve stress. This is tremendously confusing for smokers, and it is the confusion that creates the fear about quitting and that prevents us from seeing the situation as it truly is. We believe that if we have the requisite amount of willpower we will be able to muscle through these issues, but of course willpower is useless because it doesn't help the smoker to resolve the smoking dilemma and remove the desire to smoke.

As a consequence, because he hasn't changed his thinking about the cigarette and retains the desire to smoke, the willpower quitter is not really a non-smoker but a smoker who is not currently allowing himself to smoke. This is why relapse is so common among people who quit using willpower—they never remove the desire to smoke. They believe that the cigarette gave them something and that they are now depriving themselves of that something. It is this sense of deprivation and sacrifice that keeps the desire to smoke alive. Think about it, who is more likely to relapse: someone that doesn't want to smoke or someone that does?

Quite simply, the key to being a happy non-smoker is to remove the desire to smoke. With no desire to smoke, it takes no willpower not to do so. In the same way that it doesn't take you willpower not to do other things you have no desire to do. So long as willpower quitters don't understand this, they will continue to have a desire to smoke and will need to use willpower to combat that desire.

After a while of trying and failing to quit, most smokers begin to pin their hopes on the possibility—some would say fantasy—that they will suddenly wake up one morning with no desire to smoke. We hear stories and urban myths about Brett or Jane or John or Betsy to whom this happened; e.g., "I had a bout of the flu and afterwards found I didn't want to smoke any more."

Don't kid yourself. I have investigated these rumors whenever I've heard about them and they are rarely as simple as they appear. Usually the smoker has been mentally preparing himself to quit for months beforehand and uses the abstinence imposed upon him from being unwell as the trigger to launch an attempt.

More often in the case of people who stop "just like that" they have suffered some kind of shock that has jolted them into action. Perhaps a close friend or relative has just died from a smoking-related condition or they have had a scare themselves. They tell people, "I just decided to quit and that was it" because it shows them to be decisive, action-oriented, no-nonsense go-getters. Far better than admitting that you quit because you were terrified of remaining a smoker.

Please don't misunderstand me. I am not criticizing such people. Frankly, I'll support anything that helps people quit. However the problem I have with such scare tactics is that they tend not to last. As the weeks and months go by, the ex-smoker forgets how frightened they were. Because they have not removed the brainwashing or really dealt with their desire to smoke, after a period of time the cigarette begins to look attractive. Weeks or even months into their quit, they find themselves wanting to smoke and having to use willpower not to do so. Sadly, this usually ends with relapse. The ex-smoker tells themselves that they'll "just have one" to prove that they've kicked it or "to see what it's like." Of course, they get hooked even faster this time around and are left kicking themselves in anger and frustration at having fallen into the same trap again.

Let's consider in greater detail the flaws in the willpower method and why quitting using willpower (and I consider *all* other methods as willpower) is so difficult and unpleasant.

For most of our lives we bury our head in the sand about smoking, but every so often something happens which triggers an attempt to quit. As an initial step we weigh up the pros and cons of smoking. This confirms what we have known all along: by any rational assessment there is only one conclusion, STOP SMOKING!

If you were to sit down and give points out of ten to all of the advantages of stopping and do a similar exercise with the advantages of smoking, the total point count for stopping would far outweigh the count for remaining a smoker. Even hardcore smokers tend not to dispute this.

However, although the smoker knows he would be better off as a non-smoker, he believes that becoming one will involve making a tremendous sacrifice. Although this is an illusion, it is a *powerful* one. The smoker doesn't know why, but cigarettes seem to be very precious to him, and he seems to need them, in good times and in bad.

For years he has been subjected to brainwashing that cigarettes are precious, and this illusion has been reinforced by his physical addiction to nicotine, which causes him to feel uneasy when he can't smoke. On top of this he also has to deal with even more powerful brainwashing of how difficult it is to quit.

Every smoker has heard horror stories of people who have quit for months but are still desperately craving a cigarette. Then there are the bitter ex-smokers who seem intent on sharing every second of their agonizing experience with you. Smokers are also aware of the stories about people who haven't smoked for years relapsing and becoming instantly re-addicted. Anti-smoking and quit smoking TV ads showing smokers in advanced stages of cancer and emphysema, yet who cannot quit, add to the confusion. If those poor smokers can't quit, then what chance do I have?

So instead of starting this wonderful journey with a sense of excitement and anticipation, we start with a sense of doom and gloom. Sometimes we even tell our family, friends and colleagues, "Look, I'm going to try to quit so I'm going to be irritable and cranky for a few months. Try to bear with me."

So there we are, about to attack this major project, already filled with fear, misery and depression. Convinced that it's going be difficult and unpleasant and sure that we are going to fail anyway. With this frame of mind, most attempts are doomed to failure before they even start. To be honest, I find it amazing that anyone quits smoking with this approach.

Let's imagine that a willpower quitter manages to survive a few days without smoking. His mind now begins to play tricks on him. There's no physical pain, but it feels like something is missing. This feeling grows and grows and begins to obsess the smoker. We're not sure what it is we need, but we do feel sure that the cigarette will provide it. We have created a psychological need to smoke, and the only way we can overcome it is to use willpower. We try to deal with it by making an attempt not to think about smoking but, of course, this merely guarantees that you think about it even more. Soon the only thing we can think about is smoking, and we begin to say things like:

> "Life is too short. Look at September 11th. We could all die tomorrow. I could get run over by a bus. I have probably left it too late anyway. They say everything gives you cancer these days."

> "I've picked the wrong time. I should have waited until after Christmas/after the holidays/after this stressful event in my life."

> "I can't concentrate. I'm irritable and bad-tempered. I cannot do my job properly. My family and friends won't love me. Let's face it, for everybody's sake I have got to start smoking again. I'm a confirmed smoker and there is no way I will ever be happy again without a cigarette. Some people are just born to be smokers." (This one kept me smoking for thirty-three years.)

At this stage, the smoker usually admits defeat and caves in. When he lights up a kind of schizophrenia takes over. On the one hand there is the illusion of relief at being able to do something that he has been "depriving himself" of. On the other hand, the cigarette tastes awful. The smoker profoundly resents having to smoke it and can't understand why he is doing it. This is why the smoker thinks that he lacks willpower. In fact, it isn't a lack of willpower that is the problem, but a conflict of wills. It is this conflict that is at the root of the smoker's dilemma: every smoker wants to quit, but every smoker wants to keep smoking.

The smoker fails to quit not because he doesn't have enough willpower but because he has failed to resolve the conflict of wills. As a result of this failure to resolve the conflict he is forced to revert to the status quo. Given the information he has at his disposal, this is a fairly rational decision. What's the point of being healthy if you're miserable? What's the point of being rich if you're miserable? Surely it is far better to have a shorter, sweeter life than a longer, more miserable one?

Fortunately this is not true—just the reverse. Life as a non-smoker is not only longer but is infinitely more enjoyable. If this weren't true, I can assure you, I'd still be smoking and so would the 60,000,000 Americans who have already successfully quit.

The misery and the subsequent "craving" experienced by smokers trying to quit using willpower is nothing to do with physical withdrawal from nicotine. True, it is withdrawal that often triggers the misery, but the actual "craving" is a physical feeling resulting from a *mental* process, and is caused by doubt and uncertainty.

Because the smoker has started off by feeling that he is making a sacrifice, he begins to feel deprived. It can be stressful to be deprived of something we want. Because the smoker associates smoking with stress relief, as soon as he quits, he wants to smoke. However, because he is supposed to be quitting, he can't smoke, so the feeling of deprivation and misery grows. As a smoker, he would have cheered himself up with a cigarette but of course, this is the one thing he can't do, and so it goes on until finally the poor smoker puts himself out of his misery by lighting up. This dynamic explains why many willpower attempts last literally minutes.

Another problem with the willpower approach is that success is defined in negative terms. If it is your objective not to smoke for the rest of your life, then how do you know if you've succeeded until you've lived the rest of your life? This makes it hard for people using the willpower method to get closure on the smoking issue and to move on with their lives. Instead the majority of them are plagued by doubts about whether they have succeeded and about how or when they will know that they have truly broken free. This is why so many willpower quitters feel vulnerable at social occasions or during periods of stress, sometimes even years after putting out their final cigarette.

While this is truly miserable for the willpower quitter, their struggles help us to confirm that the misery or "craving" is nothing to do with nicotine. It is just not possible to continue to "crave" nicotine years after it has left their body.

These smokers are waiting for something to happen and at the same time, hoping that it won't. Desperate to smoke, but hoping they never will. This is a pretty miserable state of affairs. How much fun can it be going through life hoping nothing will happen?

As I have said, the very real misery that these willpower quitters suffer from is entirely mental and therefore (with the right mindset) entirely avoidable. It is caused by the doubt. There is no pain, but they are still obsessed with smoking. This is heartbreaking because their lives remain dominated by the cigarette, even though they are no longer smoking. If you'll excuse the crude comparison, they are the equivalent of the AA "dry drunk." It's hardly surprising that these are some of the unhappiest people you are likely to meet, or that we look at them and form a terrible fear of quitting and becoming one of them.

As the doubts fester, the fear begins to set in:

"How long will the cravings last?"

"Will I ever be happy again?"

"Will I ever want to get out of bed in the morning?"

"Will I ever enjoy a meal again?"

"How will I cope with stress?"

"Will I ever enjoy a social occasion again?"

The smoker is waiting for things to improve, but so long as he feels he is being deprived, he will remain miserable. And, of course, all the while the cigarette is looking more and more desirable.

The smoker then tells himself that he'll "just have one" and that everything will then be all right; but there is no such thing as "just one" cigarette. As soon as he puts that cigarette out, the nicotine begins to leave the body and the old empty, insecure feeling (i.e. the physical symptoms of nicotine withdrawal) re-appears. Almost immediately, a little voice at the back of his mind says, "Light another."

Fearing that he'll get hooked again (too late, he already is) he doesn't light up immediately, but waits for a few hours, days or even weeks, until he thinks it's "safe." He's on the slipperiest of slippery slopes. Most admit defeat and are soon smoking full-time again: only now they feel angry, frustrated, guilty and stupid in addition to feeling miserable.

Even smokers who succeed with the willpower method tend to find the process difficult and unpleasant and have to be constantly vigilant, often for years after they've quit. The reason for this is that they never truly get to grips with the brainwashing. Long after the physical aspect of the addiction has disappeared, the desire to smoke remains. It prolongs—sometimes indefinitely—the "cravings" and so the feeling of misery and deprivation lingers. Eventually, if he can survive for long enough without cigarettes, the willpower quitter begins to accept that life goes on and that life without cigarettes might even become tolerable. This is one of the great tragedies of the willpower quitter—they never get to celebrate their achievement and to enjoy their freedom from the slavery of smoking.

It's true that many people stop smoking using willpower, but I feel that this does not, on its own, define success. True success in the smoking cessation context is when you are *happy* to be a non-smoker, and when you are able to enjoy the health, happiness and freedom to which this most wonderful of achievements entitles you.

The truth is that with willpower, there are far more failures than successes. According to the journal *Tobacco Control*, twelve-month success rates using pure willpower with no education, motivation or support range from 2–5%. Success rates for other popular quit methods are difficult to gauge, but studies show real-life quit rates of around 7% for Nicotine Replacement Therapy (patches, nicotine gum etc.) and 12–15% for Zyban (Wellbutrin) and 15% for the latest "wonder drug" Champix. Links to these studies can be found on our US website: www.TheEasywayToStopSmoking.com

Looking at it another way, the most "successful" variant of the willpower approach has an 85% failure rate at twelve months and the least successful a 95% failure rate. Our seminar centers would close in a month if they delivered these kinds of results.

The reason for this lack of success with the willpower approach is obvious to me. It doesn't help smokers understand why they smoke, or deal with the psychological desire to light up. So long as the desire to smoke remains, the smoker will struggle to break free. The desire can and does remain with many willpower quitters for the rest of their lives, and this explains why they remain so vulnerable even years after they've quit.

They continue to believe that they enjoy smoking, but that they have deprived themselves by quitting. As I have often said, enjoyment doesn't come into it. It never did! If enjoyment were the reason that people smoked, no one would smoke more than one. We assume that we enjoy them because we have to. We'd feel stupid if we continued to smoke and did not "enjoy" it. That's why many of the cigarettes we smoke, we're barely even aware we're smoking. If every time we lit up we had to be acutely aware of the smell, the taste, the consequences and that this might be the one that triggers the lung cancer, then even the illusion of enjoyment would disappear.

Watch smokers when you get a chance. It's clear that they don't particularly enjoy it. You'll see that they are only happy when they are not aware they're smoking. Once they become aware they get uncomfortable, self-conscious and apologetic.

Keep it simple. We smoke to feed that "little nicotine monster." Once you have purged him from your body and the brainwashing from your mind, you'll have neither the need nor the desire to smoke.

CHAPTER 23

BEWARE OF CUTTING DOWN

Many smokers resort to cutting down either as a stepping stone towards quitting or as an attempt to control the "little monster." Only people who have never smoked a cigarette in their life endorse this strategy.

As a stepping stone to stopping, cutting down is fatal. It is our attempts to cut down that can keep us trapped for life.

Usually, cutting down follows a failed attempt to stop. After a few hours or days of abstinence using willpower, the smoker says something like, "There's no way I can quit so I'll cut down and just smoke the special ones."

Terrible things happen.

- You keep the "little monster" alive wanting to be fed as before, but now you are only feeding him on a restricted basis. This forces you to experience the "big monster"—the psychological "craving" to smoke—more often and with more intensity.

- You spend your whole life looking at your watch, wishing your life away waiting for the next cigarette.
- You have the worst of all worlds. You have to use will-power as if you were quitting, but for all your effort and trouble, you don't even get to be a non-smoker!

When you smoke as much as you want you rarely feel that you enjoy any of them. You're smoking because it's just what you do. However, when you cut down, self-imposed abstinence creates the feeling that every cigarette is precious.

Again, all this is obvious when you think about it. When we cut down, we are abstaining from smoking whenever we want. We still have the desire to smoke say, every forty-five minutes, but we are limiting ourselves to one every couple of hours. During that time, our desire to smoke builds, and the longer we wait to scratch the "itch," the more "enjoyable" it seems when we can at last scratch it.

Of course, this is also an illusion because what we are "enjoying" when we smoke after a period of abstinence is not the cigarette, but ending the state of wanting or needing it. This is evident throughout our smoking lives. So many "special" cigarettes come after a period of abstinence—the first of the day, the one after a meal, the one after a long flight, and so on. The longer the perceived period of "suffering" between cigarettes the greater the illusion of relief or "pleasure" when we can finally light up.

The main difficulty of stopping smoking is not the chemical aspect of the addiction. That's easy. Smokers go through nicotine withdrawal every night when they go to sleep and it doesn't bother them in the slightest. The "cravings" that terrify us so profoundly are, in fact, so mild they don't even wake you up. In the morning, most smokers will actually leave the bedroom before lighting up. Many will eat breakfast. Because so few people smoke in their homes these days, many will wait until they're on their way to work before lighting up.

Most smokers go between eight and ten hours every night without a cigarette and it doesn't bother them. Interestingly, many of them couldn't do this during the day. They'd be tearing their hair out. Yet the withdrawal we experience is identical, regardless of whether we're awake or asleep.

No, our obsession with the chemical side of the addiction is misplaced. The real problem is psychological. Ironically, all smokers and nearly all doctors know this, yet still we are told that the solution is a pill or a patch. I have yet to come across another field of medicine where the success rates for pharmacological treatments are so poor yet they remain the supposed "gold standard" of treatment.

The real challenge that smokers face is to counter the brainwashing to which we all have been exposed. A major part of the brainwashing is the idea of the cigarette as a reward or special treat or crutch. Cutting down reinforces this illusion. It leaves you feeling miserable and deprived for extended periods (i.e. when you are abstaining) and this convinces you that the most precious thing on earth is the next cigarette. Even though we might smoke less for a time (in my experience, cutting down never lasted more than a day or so), but during that time you are more enslaved than ever. The cigarette dominates your whole life.

There is nothing sadder than the smoker who is trying to cut down. He suffers from the drug addict's delusion that the less he smokes, the less he will want to smoke. In fact, the reverse is true. The less he smokes, the longer he endures the psychological itch to smoke and the more he treasures finally being able to scratch that itch.

A slightly odd twist to cutting down is that the smoker often becomes more aware of the taste, which he invariably finds distasteful. It doesn't stop him smoking, but he does begin to wonder why he is doing it. Like chemical addiction, taste is a red herring. We often find that our most precious cigarettes are the ones that taste the most foul. The first of the day is a classic example. For many smokers, the first of the day is the most important of all, yet it's the one that has them coughing and spluttering the most.

It is essential to remove all the illusions about smoking before you smoke a final cigarette. Unless you've removed the illusion that you enjoy the taste of certain cigarettes, there will be no way of proving it after you become a non-smoker without getting hooked again. So, unless you are already smoking, light one up now. Take six big drags, inhaling each drag as deeply into your lungs as you can. Now ask yourself what it is about the taste that you enjoy.

Perhaps, as I did, you believe that only certain cigarettes taste good, like the one after a meal. If this was so, then why smoke the others? Anyway, how can two cigarettes from the same pack taste different?

Don't take my word for it; see for yourself. Smoke a cigarette consciously after a meal to see if it tastes different to the others. The reason that the smoker perceives that the one after a meal or at a social occasion is more enjoyable, is because at such times we are enjoying ourselves anyway, whether we're a smoker or not. The one after a meal is for some people the most precious of all. This is because in addition to being at a time when we're having fun anyway, it also comes after a period of abstinence.

It is such a shame that smokers so value the one after a meal when the truth is that they should be acknowledging that it is their need to smoke that has ruined their ability to enjoy the meal in the first place.

As I have said many times: It's not that we enjoy smoking, it's that we're miserable when we can't smoke. But non-smokers don't get miserable when they can't smoke. The cigarette causes the misery. Why can't we see this when it is so obvious to everyone else?

Cutting down not only doesn't work, but it is also the worst form of torture. It doesn't work because smoking is not a habit, it is an addiction. You can't become less addicted to something, you're either addicted or you are not. We can't break a pack-a-day addiction and re-make it as a two-a-day addiction. You aren't deciding how much you will smoke; the rate at which your body metabolizes nicotine dictates how much you will smoke.

When we cut down, our psychological "need" to smoke remains the same but now we are only servicing that need on a limited basis. This means that we spend large amounts of time wanting to smoke but not allowing ourselves to do so. This builds a feeling of deprivation and sacrifice identical to that experienced by the smoker trying to quit using willpower. Therefore when we are cutting down, we have to suffer the misery of the willpower quitter without even getting the benefit of being smoke-free! It is truly the worst of both worlds. You have to apply willpower and discipline for the rest of your life. Who could think of a more miserable future?

As I said, the main problem with stopping is not the chemical addiction, but the mistaken belief that the cigarette gives you some pleasure and that as a non-smoker you will be depriving yourself of that pleasure. This mistaken belief is triggered by the brainwashing we are subjected to before we become smokers, and is reinforced by the chemical addiction once we do. All cutting down does is to reinforce this fallacy further to the extent that smoking comes to dominate the smoker's life and convince him that the most precious thing on the planet is the next cigarette.

In any case, as I've already said, cutting down doesn't work anyway. It takes enormous amounts of willpower to cut down. If you haven't had the willpower to quit, why do you think you'll have the much larger amount of willpower needed to cut down?

Through all the smokers and ex-smokers I have met, I have heard of literally tens of thousands of attempts to quit by cutting down. I have only heard of a handful of successes. Of all the quit smoking techniques this has to be the least successful and the most unpleasant. I wouldn't wish it on my worst enemy.

However, the experience of cutting down does help us to explode one of the myths about smoking because it clearly illustrates that smoking is only "pleasurable" after a period of abstinence. Once you see that, it becomes very obvious that we are not enjoying the cigarette itself, but the ending of the state of misery of needing it.

So your choices are simple:

Cut down for life. This is self-imposed torture and you will fail miserably (as have millions of smokers before you) because smoking isn't a habit that you can break and re-make in another form, but drug addiction. "Cutting down" doesn't work with drug addiction!

Continue to smoke as you do now, being dominated by fear, misery and slavery. What is the point?

Break free, take your life back and give yourself the gifts of health, happiness and freedom.

The other important point that cutting down demonstrates is that there is no such thing as "just one" cigarette. Smoking is a chain reaction. Every cigarette creates the "need" to smoke the next. You can't break the chain by cutting down, only by breaking the chain!

REMEMBER: CUTTING DOWN WILL DRAG YOU DOWN.

CHAPTER 24

JUST ONE CIGARETTE

"Just one cigarette" is a myth you must get out of your mind. See it for what it really is—fiction.

It is "just one cigarette" that gets us hooked in the first place. That "one" cigarette led to the tens of thousands of others you have smoked.

It is "just one cigarette" to tide us over a difficult patch or on a special occasion that is the cause of failure of most of our attempts to stop.

It is "just one cigarette" that, when smokers think they are free, sends them back into the trap. Sometimes we smoke it just to confirm that we have indeed broken free. It tastes horrible and you question how you could have become hooked in the first place. You are convinced you could never get hooked again, but you already are. Before you know it, you're back buying cigarettes and wondering what on earth happened.

It is the thought of that one "special" cigarette that often prevents smokers from even trying to stop: the first in the morning or the one after a meal.

Get it firmly into your mind that there is no such thing as "just one cigarette." It is a chain reaction that will dominate you for the rest of your life unless you choose to break it.

It is the myth of the occasional or "special" cigarette that keeps willpower quitters mourning the loss of their "little friend" instead of celebrating the death of an enemy. You must teach yourself to see smoking for what it really is. That "just one cigarette" led to the years and years of slavery and torture you have had to endure as a smoker.

Whenever you think about smoking you must see it as a lifetime's chain of filth, disease, fear, misery and slavery. These are the facts of smoking. A lifetime of paying an exorbitant amount of money for the privilege of feeding yourself poison. A lifetime of shame, anger, guilt, bad breath, and mental and physical torture. And for what do we put ourselves through this awful experience? So we can remove the slightly empty feeling of withdrawal caused by the previous cigarette, and feel like a non-smoker.

There are two things in particular that really grind us down about smoking. First, it's so unremitting. The cigarette has got you by the throat and, so long as you remain a smoker, it never lets go. You never get a day off, or even a couple of hours off. It doesn't matter if it's twenty below outside, or if you have a cough or a cold, or if you're on a plane or at the movies—it never lets up and gives you a break.

The second is that it's so unrewarding. It's only when we are not smoking that the cigarette seems desirable. When we're smoking we're mostly either unaware of it or we are aware but wishing we didn't have to. All the cigarette does is remove the need to smoke and in doing so, momentarily lets you feel like a non-smoker.

If you struggle with this, ask yourself a simple question. If you could go back in time to when you smoked your first cigarette and you had the knowledge, understanding and experience of smoking you have now, would you still light that cigarette? Every smoker on the planet would answer the same: "You have got to be joking!" Yet every smoker has this choice every day of his smoking life. Why don't we opt for what we know to be the smart choice? The answer is fear: the fear that we'll be unable to enjoy life or cope with stress. We ignore the fact that we are not enjoying life as a smoker and that the cigarette itself is causing the stress.

Stop selling yourself short. You can do this. Anybody can. It's ridiculously easy.

In order to make it easy to stop smoking there are certain fundamentals to get clear in your mind. We have already dealt with three of them up to now:

- There is nothing to give up. On the contrary, by quitting you are earning yourself the wonderful gifts of health, happiness and freedom.

- There is no such thing as "just one cigarette"; just a lifetime's chain of filth, disease and misery. Your very first cigarette led to every single cigarette you have ever smoked.

- In a smoking context, there is nothing unique or different about you. All smokers fell into the same trap, and with the right information and mindset, all smokers can find it easy to stop.

Many believe that they are confirmed smokers or have "addictive personalities," but I'm not so sure. No one needed to smoke before they lit that first cigarette and became hooked. It is the effect of all drugs to make us feel powerless and helpless.

This makes us want the drug more so that we can remove the feeling and once again feel normal. It is the drug that addicts us, not our personalities. These feelings of frailty and that we are somehow flawed and incomplete are promoted aggressively by advertisers in a wide range of categories, who use these fears to sell their products.

It is essential to remove this belief that we are helplessly dependent on nicotine (or any other drug for that matter). The reason for this is that if we believe it, it becomes our reality. Up to now we have believed ourselves to be dependent on cigarettes but the truth is that it is the cigarette itself that creates the "need" to smoke. Non-smokers don't have it.

If we can replace the fear with facts, we can see the cigarette for what it really is—a nicotine delivery device—and remove the belief that we "need" to smoke. With no "need" to smoke or desire to do so, it's easy to break free. It is essential to remove all the brainwashing.

CHAPTER 25

CASUAL SMOKERS, TEENAGERS, NON-SMOKERS

Heavy smokers tend to envy casual smokers. We've all met these characters: "Oh, I can go all week without a cigarette, it really doesn't bother me." We think: "I wish I were like that." I know this is hard to believe, but there is no such thing as a happy smoker—casual or otherwise. No smoker enjoys being a smoker. Never forget:

No smoker decided that they were going to become a smoker—casual or otherwise. They fell into a trap.

Some smokers find it difficult to admit to themselves that they have fallen for a trap because to do so would be to admit to a flaw or weakness, so they are in denial.

They lie to themselves and others about their smoking in an attempt to justify what they know to be thoroughly irrational behavior.

I used to be a fanatical golfer. Because I enjoyed it so much I would play whenever I could. If casual smokers think that smoking is so enjoyable, why don't they do it more? And why do casual smokers feel bound to say things like "I could go all week without a smoke and it wouldn't bother me." Why bother to say such a thing? If I said: "I could go a whole week without a carrot" would you think that I didn't have a problem with carrots, or that I did? If I didn't have a problem with carrots, why would I be telling you about how masterfully I can control my intake of them? It doesn't add up.

The casual smoker is trying to convince both of you that he doesn't have a problem. But if he didn't have a problem, surely he wouldn't have a need to mention it? After all, I'm sure you don't go around telling people that you can go all week without shooting up with heroin. Why make such a statement unless you are a heroin addict? Only a heroin addict would be proud of going without, all week.

It doesn't make sense. Casual smokers would have you believe that they could take or leave cigarettes. But if this were true, why would they take them? Which adult, knowing what we know now about smoking, would choose to become a smoker? Would you?

Actually, I believe many casual smokers are more firmly hooked than heavy smokers. The reason for this is that they suffer from the illusion that they enjoy smoking, whereas few heavy smokers believe they enjoy smoking—they are just doing it because they don't think they can stop.

Remember, the only "pleasure" that smokers get is the illusory one of temporarily relieving the very slight withdrawal symptoms caused by the previous cigarette. Picture that little nicotine monster as an itch. For the most part, it is so slight we are barely even aware of it.

All smokers, casual or otherwise, have this "itch" and of course the natural tendency is to scratch it as soon as you become aware of it. By lighting up, we scratch the itch, but because our bodies build immunity to the effect of the drug, as time goes on we tend to need to smoke more to relieve it. Soon, nicotine withdrawal creates a permanent itch, and this is why most smokers become regular smokers, and also why some become chain-smokers.

Casual smokers remain so for a variety of reasons:

- FEAR: They are terrified of the consequences of smoking more and think that by limiting their intake they are limiting their risk.
- MONEY: They physically can't afford to smoke more, or resent paying for something they don't enjoy, so they limit their intake in an attempt to control the cost.
- LACK OF OPPORTUNITY: These days many people won't smoke in their car, at work, at home or when their kids are around. This only leaves a very limited number of opportunities to smoke and so these smokers have to use significant amounts of willpower not to smoke more.
- FEAR OF LOSS OF CONTROL: These people hate smoking and being a smoker. They live in fear of becoming hooked, but of course, already are.

I used to think of my chain-smoking as a weakness. I couldn't understand why my friends could limit their intake to five, ten or twenty a day. I knew I was a very strong-willed person. It never occurred to me that most smokers are physically incapable of chain-smoking. The truth is that these five-a-day smokers whom I envied throughout my smoking life don't smoke more because their bodies can't hack it, they detest it, they can't afford to, they are using willpower not to or they are terrified of the consequences.

Let's take a closer look at the different categories of "casual" smoker.

THE BEGINNER. This is the teenager who is trying the odd cigarette at parties or when hanging out with their friends. At this stage, the cigarette tastes absolutely disgusting and the teenager is convinced that he could never get hooked. Unfortunately this is exactly how and when over 95% of us became addicted and we spend the rest of our lives paying for it and trying to break free.

THE RELAPSER. This is a smoker who was previously a heavier smoker but feels he can't do without altogether. This smoker usually falls into a couple of categories:

> *The five-a-day smoker:* I envied these people my whole smoking life. It never occurred to me how unhappy they were. If they enjoy smoking, why not smoke more? If they don't enjoy it, then why smoke at all? This smoker is relieving the withdrawal pangs for less than an hour a day. For the rest of the day he is in withdrawal and having to use willpower not to scratch the itch.

> *The morning-only or evening-only smoker:* He punishes himself by suffering withdrawal and using willpower for half the day so that he can relieve his perceived need to smoke for the other half. This is like banging your head against a brick wall because it feels better when you stop.

> *The six-months-on, six-months-off smoker:* (Or the "I can stop whenever I want" smoker). If he enjoys smoking, then why does he want to stop? If he doesn't enjoy it, why does he start again? The truth is that this smoker is hooked twelve months of the year. When he smokes he feels lethargic and trapped and after six months he feels so bad that he needs to stop. As a non-smoker, he feels much better, but over time forgets what it felt like to

have to be a smoker and, because he has never dealt with the brainwashing, senses that he is depriving himself or missing out on something. So he lights a cigarette. It's pretty disgusting so he falls for the same trap as the teenager. ("I could never get hooked on something as disgusting as this!") Before he knows it, he is buying cigarettes again and the whole cycle repeats. Many smokers envy these types of smokers, but in many ways they are the saddest of all. When they are smokers they wish they were non-smokers and when they are non-smokers they are wishing they could smoke. That's not a life, it's a nightmare.

The "I only smoke on special occasions" smoker: Isn't it amazing how everything seems to be a special occasion?

The "I've stopped but I'll have the occasional smoke" smoker: This goes back to the "just one" cigarette argument. These smokers are headed back to full-time smoking. Think about it this way: if a recovering alcoholic came to your house and said that he was "just going to have one drink" what would you advise? Nicotine is many, many times more addictive than alcohol.

There are two other categories of casual smoker. The first is the type who smokes the very occasional cigarette or cigar, almost always at social occasions. These people are really non-smokers but sense that they might be missing out on something. If you look closely, it's clear that they're hating every second of it. They often don't inhale and look awkward or uncomfortable when they are smoking. They just don't "get" smoking but can't believe that the smoker isn't enjoying it. If they are adults, they often just give up trying to enjoy it and the whole world of smoking remains an inexplicable mystery to them. If they are teenagers, many of them will persist with smoking in the mistaken belief that there must be something to it, and that they could never get hooked anyway. We all started this way.

The second category is very rare indeed. In fact, out of all the smokers who have sought my assistance, I can only think of about a dozen examples. The type can best be described by outlining a recent case.

A woman phoned our center and insisted on speaking to me personally. She was seeking a private session. She is an attorney, had only been smoking for about twelve years and had never smoked more or less than two cigarettes a day. She was, it was clear, a very intelligent and strong-willed lady. I explained that the success rate in group sessions was just as high as in private sessions, and in any event I was only able to give individual therapy if the attendee's face were so famous that it would disrupt the rest of the group. She began to cry, and I was not able to resist the tears.

The session was expensive. Actually, most smokers would wonder why she wanted to stop in the first place. They would gladly pay me double what that lady did to be able to smoke only two cigarettes a day. However, in doing so they would be making the mistake of assuming that seemingly "casual" smokers like my client are happier and more in control. In this woman's case both her parents had died from lung cancer before she herself had started smoking. Like me, she had a terrible fear of smoking before she started. Like me, she eventually caved in under the massive brainwashing and tried her first cigarette. Like me, she can remember the foul taste. Unlike me, who capitulated and became a chain-smoker very quickly, she resisted the slide.

All any smoker ever "enjoys" in a cigarette is the ending of the state of "needing" it. This is irrespective of whether or not it is the barely perceptible physical itch, or the much greater psychological torture of not being able to scratch it. Cigarettes themselves are filth and poison. This is why we only have the illusion of enjoyment after a period of abstinence. Just like thirst or hunger, the longer you experience it, the greater the sense of relief.

Smokers make the mistake of believing that smoking is a "habit." They think that if they can reduce their intake and maintain it at that level, then they can break their old "habit" and replace it with a new one. But smoking is not a habit; it's drug addiction.

When you have an itch, the natural tendency is to scratch it. With cigarettes, as your body creates immunity to nicotine over the years, you need to smoke more to relieve the "itch." The more you smoke, the less effect each cigarette has, and the more you need to smoke. As the drug begins to destroy you physically and mentally, as it gradually eats away at your nervous system and your confidence and courage, you are increasingly unable to limit the interval between each cigarette. This explains why people like me, who never even have any illusion that they enjoy smoking, end up as chain-smokers, even though you hate it and every cigarette is torture.

Back to the female attorney: ironically, most smokers would envy her and would be staggered to hear the misery that this poor woman had to endure. When you only smoke one cigarette every twelve hours, it appears to be the most precious thing on earth. For twelve years that poor woman was at the center of a tug-of-war. She had been unable to stop smoking but was terrified of getting lung cancer like her parents. For twenty-three hours and fifty minutes a day, she had to use willpower to fight the temptation to smoke. For the ten minutes of the day she was smoking, she felt guilt, fear, self-loathing, anger and frustration. This poor woman smoked two cigarettes a day, but her whole life was dominated by those two cigarettes. So much for "casual" smoking.

I remember another case, the man who was the inspiration for this book, who was a five-a-day smoker. He called me and started to tell his story in the croaky voice I know to be the voice of a throat cancer victim. He said: "Mr. Carr, I just want to stop smoking before I die." This is how he described his life:

"I am sixty-one years old. I have cancer of the throat through smoking. Now I can only physically cope with five roll-ups a day. I used to sleep soundly through the night. Now I wake up every hour of the night and all I can think about is cigarettes. Even when I am sleeping, I dream about smoking.

"I cannot have my first cigarette until ten o'clock. I get up at five o'clock and make endless cups of tea. My wife gets up about eight o'clock and, because I am so bad-tempered, she will not have me in the house. I go down to the greenhouse and try to potter about, but my mind is obsessed with smoking. At nine o'clock I begin to roll my first cigarette and I do so until it is perfect. It is not that I need it to be perfect, but it gives me something to do. I then wait for ten o'clock. When it arrives my hands are shaking uncontrollably. I do not light the cigarette then. If I do, I have to wait three hours for the next one. Eventually I light the cigarette, take one puff and extinguish it immediately. By continuing this process I can make the cigarette last an hour. I smoke it down to about a quarter of an inch and then wait for the next one."

In addition to his other troubles, this poor man had burns all over his lips caused by smoking the cigarette too low. Reading this, you probably have visions of a weak-willed jellyfish of a man. Not so. This man was over six feet tall and a decorated ex-Marine. He was a former athlete and didn't want to become a smoker. However, in World War II, cigarettes were provided free of charge as part of every soldier's rations. This man was virtually ordered to become a smoker and he has spent the rest of his life paying. By the time he contacted me, he was a mental, physical and nervous wreck, all due to smoking and the stranglehold the cigarette had on this tragic hero's life. Had he been an animal, our society would have had him put down as a mercy killing.

You may think the above case is exaggerated. It is extreme but not unique. That man poured his heart out to me, but you can be sure that many of his friends and acquaintances envied him for being a five-a-day man.

Isn't it strange that, as smokers, we equate smoking less with being happier, yet we perceive not smoking at all as terrifying? It doesn't seem to occur to us that the obvious conclusion is that the cigarette creates the misery in the first place. It also eludes us that using this rationale the happiest people would be non-smokers. These points are very obvious to non-smokers but fear prevents smokers from accepting them.

The truth is that casual smokers are no happier than heavy smokers, and many of them are extremely unhappy indeed. The manifestation of their addiction is a little different to that of the regular smoker, but they are addicted nonetheless. As casual smokers they suffer from two additional burdens that make their lives even more miserable. Firstly, they are only servicing their addiction on a limited basis. This means that they have to use willpower and go through extended periods of enduring the torture of wanting to smoke but not allowing themselves to do so. Second, because they are abstaining on a prolonged basis, they suffer from the illusion that they enjoy smoking where in fact they are enjoying an end to the dissatisfied state of needing to smoke.

In any case, drug addicts are notorious liars and this includes many "casual" smokers. Most "casual" smokers smoke far more and far more frequently than they care to admit. I have lost count of the number of conversations I have had with so-called five-a-day smokers who have smoked more than five during the course of the conversation! Observe "casual" smokers at social occasions such as weddings and parties. They'll be chain-smoking along with the best of them.

You don't need to envy casual smokers. The truth is that they, along with all of the other smokers in your life, will be envying you when you break free. Life is so much sweeter without dragging this ball and chain with you wherever you go.

Teenagers can be more of a challenge to cure because they don't believe that they are hooked and they think they could quit anytime they wanted to. By the time they work it all out; it's too late. I'd like to warn the parents of children who loathe smoking not to have a false sense of security. All children hate smoking right up until the time they become hooked.

It saddens and frustrates me that, despite investing tens of millions of dollars, society has still not found an effective way to prevent children from starting to smoke. Health warnings don't deter young people because teenagers think the warnings are only applicable to older smokers. They treat the anti-smoking education programs like DARE (Drug Abuse Resistance Education) as a joke. Attempts by the establishment to deter kids from smoking only serve to make it appear more desirable. The reason for this is that the children are receiving mixed messages. On the one hand, very un-cool people (teachers, doctors, health educators) are telling them that it is not cool to smoke. But on the other hand, very cool people (peers, older kids, movie stars, rock stars) are telling them that it is very cool to smoke. Put yourself in a thirteen-year-old's place; which story would you buy?

What I find genuinely difficult to accept is that we continue to allow tobacco companies and their proxies to promote tobacco to children. According to the *Smoke Free Movies* website, between May 2002 and April 2003, 82% of top grossing PG-13 films featured smoking scenes and half of all the smoking shots were in movies rated for kids. This is up substantially from 1999–2000, when only 21% of the tobacco shots were in movies rated G, PG, and PG13. People tend to be shocked and horrified at such data, but there's really nothing new here. Hollywood has always been a key channel for the promotion of the smoking message, going back to the days of Dietrich, Bogart and Spencer Tracy.

It is an irrefutable fact that the vast majority of youngsters who end up addicted to cocaine, heroin or any other of the so-called hard drugs, are introduced to the concept of addiction by smoking tobacco. I have yet to meet a heroin addict who was not first a smoker. If you can help your children to avoid the smoking trap, you substantially reduce the risk of them becoming dependent on heavier drugs. As a smoker you are a walking, talking, real-life billboard for smoking. Being free from that role is a wonderful bonus when you become a happy non-smoker.

CHAPTER 26

THE SECRET SMOKER

The secret smoker should be grouped with casual smokers, but the effects of secret smoking are so insidious that it merits a separate chapter. It can lead to the breakdown of personal relationships. In my case it nearly caused a divorce.

I was three weeks into one of my failed attempts to stop. The attempt had been triggered by my wife's worry about my constant wheezing and coughing. I had told her I was not worried about my health. She said, "I know you aren't, but how would you feel if you had to watch someone you love systematically destroying themselves?" It was an argument that I found irresistible, hence the attempt to stop. The attempt ended at around the three-week mark after a heated argument with an old friend. It did not register until years afterwards that my devious mind had deliberately triggered the argument. I felt justly aggrieved at the time, but I do not believe that it was coincidence, as I had never argued with this particular friend before, nor have I since. Anyway, I had my excuse. I desperately "needed" a cigarette and started smoking again.

I could not bear to think of the disappointment this would cause my wife, so I didn't tell her. I just smoked when alone. Then gradually I started smoking in the company of friends until it got to the point where everybody knew I was smoking except my wife. I remember being quite pleased at the time. I thought, "Well, at least it is cutting my consumption down." Eventually she accused me of continuing to smoke. She described the times I had caused an argument and stormed out of the house or taken two hours to go out and purchase some minor item, and the occasions when I would normally have invited her to accompany me and had made feeble excuses to go alone.

As the antisocial split between smokers and non-smokers widens, there are literally thousands of cases where the company of friends or relatives is restricted or avoided altogether because of this awful weed. The worst thing about secret smoking is that it reinforces the fallacy in the smoker's mind that he is being deprived. At the same time, it causes a major loss of self-respect as otherwise honest, decent folk are forced to deceive those whom they love the most. This happened to me on several occasions and I am sure it has also happened to you.

I remember the 1970s detective show, *Columbo,* starring Peter Falk. The theme of each episode is similar. The villain, usually a wealthy and respected businessman, has committed what he thinks is the perfect murder and his confidence in remaining undetected as the perpetrator receives a boost when the shabby-looking and seemingly disorganized Columbo is assigned to the case.

Columbo has this frustrating practice of closing the door after finishing his interrogation, having assured the suspect that he is in the clear, and before the satisfied smirk has left the murderer's face, Columbo reappears with: "Just one small point, sir, which I'm sure you can explain..." The suspect stammers, and from that point on we know and he knows that Columbo will gradually wear him down.

No matter how awful the crime, from that point on my sympathies were with the murderer. As a secret smoker, I felt like a criminal. The endless hours of not being able to smoke, then sneaking out into the garage for a desperation drag or two, shivering in the cold wondering where the pleasure was. The fear of being caught red-handed like a naughty school-boy. Would Joyce discover where I had hidden the cigarettes, lighter and butts? The relief of returning to the house undiscovered only to begin to panic about whether she would smell the smoke on my breath or clothes. As I took longer and more frequent absences, the risk increased. I knew that it was only a matter of time until I was discovered. The final humiliation and shame almost came as a relief as the sheer torture of being a secret smoker was replaced by the very slightly more tolerable torture of once again becoming a chain-smoker.

OH, THE JOYS OF BEING A SMOKER!

CHAPTER 27

A SOCIAL HABIT?

The main reason there are now far more ex-smokers than smokers in the US is the social revolution that is taking place with respect to smoking.

Yes, I know: health and money are the main reasons that smokers quote as their motivation to quit, but this has always been the case and doesn't totally explain the very rapid decline in smoking rates. Smokers have lived with the health risks for decades. You don't need cancer scares or health warnings to know that cigarettes ruin your life. These bodies of ours are the most sophisticated machines on the planet and they tell us—no, they practically yell at us—from the first drag to the last that cigarettes are POISON.

The only reason we get dragged into it in the first place is because of the social pressure from our friends or siblings. Smoking was once considered to be a social lubricant and, to a degree, it still is by teenagers, mainly for the reasons explained in Chapter 25. But today, even most smokers acknowledge that smoking is antisocial. When I was a smoker you could still light up in most places including offices, trains, pubs, clubs, cinemas and even friend's houses. In those days the cigarette was the proud badge of the tough guy and the sophisticated lady.

Today the situation couldn't be more different. Everyone knows that the only reason that smokers smoke is because they have failed to stop or they are too frightened to even try. Increasingly the smoker is marginalized and demonized by society. Apart from glass-walled airport "smoking rooms" designed to humiliate the smoker and put him on display like a circus attraction, there are few indoor places for smokers to smoke. Even bars are choosing or being forced to go smoke-free. Smokers are sent outside in the wind and the rain and bitter cold. A traumatized smoker called to book into our Los Angeles seminar because someone had actually spat at her when she was smoking on the sidewalk. A New York woman—a beautiful, classy and elegant woman in her fifties, called to make a reservation after she had been asked to smoke in the alley behind a restaurant where she was eating, along with the trash cans and the rats.

This revolution is changing the way society looks at smokers and the way smokers see themselves. I've recently seen situations that I remember as a boy but I haven't seen for years—like smokers flicking ash into their cupped hand or even their pocket because they are too embarrassed to ask for an ashtray.

I was in a restaurant years ago. It was midnight and everyone had long since stopped eating. At a time when the cigarettes and cigars are usually rife, not one person was smoking. I assumed that it must be a non-smoking restaurant but when I asked the waiter he said that they had no restrictions on smoking. Just as we were talking, someone lit up. That plume of smoke triggered a sequence of beacons through the restaurant. All the smokers had been sitting there thinking, "Surely I can't be the only smoker," suffering in silence and too ashamed to light up.

What was once a social habit has become a source of shame and embarrassment. And it's not getting better. Though it's difficult to imagine, things will continue to get worse for smokers in the US. There isn't a city or town that doesn't have draconian smoking by-laws or plans to implement them. There is even talk of legislation to attempt to ban smoking in private homes and cars if those spaces are shared with non-smokers.

Every day more and more smokers leave this sinking ship. In a 2008 Gallup poll, over three-quarters of current smokers wanted to quit. As smokers give up in droves, those left in the trap begin to worry about being left on their own.

DON'T LET IT BE YOU!

CHAPTER 28

TIMING

Apart from the obvious point that as it is doing you no good, now is the right time to stop, I believe timing to be one of the most important aspects of quitting.

Our society, despite its professed hatred of smoking, doesn't take it all *that* seriously though. Society tends to treat smoking as a bad habit that has unfortunate side effects with respect to health. This is a bit like saying that Tiger Woods is a decent golfer—something of an understatement. Over one billion people (including over fifty million people in North America) are addicted to nicotine. Smoking kills around five million people every year, including an estimated 450,000 Americans. It is, by far, the leading cause of preventable death in every developed country in the world. For many smokers, their one biggest regret in life was lighting their first cigarette.

The figures quoted above provide ample demonstration, if any were needed, that the stakes are very high. Your health, happiness and freedom are at stake. If you don't get this right, you could pay with your life, as five million smokers did last year, and five million more will next year. It is important to do everything you can to give yourself the best possible chance of success and this means getting the timing right.

First of all, identify the times when smoking appears most important to you. If you are a businessman and smoke for the illusion of stress relief, choose a relatively slack period, or perhaps your annual vacation. If you think you smoke mainly when you are bored, choose a time when you know you'll be busy.

Look a few weeks into the future and try to anticipate whether there might be an occasion or event that might cause you to fail. Occasions like weddings or Christmas need not deter you, so long as you anticipate them in advance and do not feel you will be deprived. Do NOT attempt to cut down in the meantime, as this will only create the illusion that the cigarette is enjoyable as explained in Chapter 23. If anything, it helps to force as many of the filthy things down you as possible. This removes even the illusion of pleasure. While you are smoking your last cigarettes be aware of the disgusting smell and taste and think how wonderful it will be when finally you allow yourself to stop doing it.

WHATEVER YOU DO, DON'T FALL INTO THE TRAP OF PROCRASTINATING AND PUTTING IT OUT OF YOUR MIND. FINALIZE YOUR TIMETABLE NOW AND LOOK FORWARD TO IT. Remember you aren't giving anything up. On the contrary: you are about to receive marvelous positive gains.

For years I've been saying that I know as much about the mysteries of quitting smoking as anyone else on the planet. The problem is this: although every smoker smokes purely to relieve the chemical withdrawal created by the previous cigarette, it is not the nicotine addiction itself that hooks the smoker but the brainwashing that results from that addiction. Every individual smoker has his or her own individualized version of the brainwashing. In most aspects of the smoking puzzle these differences don't matter but in the area of timing they can be critical.

With the benefit of the many years of feedback that I have received since the original publication of this book, and bearing in mind that each day I learn something new about smoking, I was agreeably surprised to realize that the philosophy I propounded in the first edition was still sound. I know for a fact that with the right mindset, every smoker can find it not only easy to stop but can actually enjoy the process. Unfortunately, knowing this is useless unless I can communicate it to smokers. And unless I can make them believe it, they will continue to believe that quitting has to be tough and unpleasant.

Many people have said to me: "You say, 'Continue to smoke until you have finished the book.' This makes people read the book slowly or just not finish it at all. You should change that instruction." This sounds logical, but I know that if the instruction were to stop immediately, some smokers wouldn't even start reading the book.

I had a smoker consult me in the early days. He said, "I really resent having to seek your help. I know I'm a strong-willed person. In every other area of my life I'm in control. Why is it that all these other smokers are stopping by using their own willpower, yet I have to come to you?" He continued, "I think I could do it on my own, if I could smoke while I was doing it."

This may sound like a contradiction, but I know what the man meant. We think of stopping smoking as something that is very difficult and unpleasant. What do we need when we have something difficult to do? We need our "little friend." So stopping smoking seems to the smoker to be a double blow. Not only do we have something we perceive to be difficult and unpleasant to do, but we also have to do without our crutch while we're doing it.

It didn't occur to me until long after that man had left that my instruction to keep smoking is the real beauty of the Easyway method. You can continue to smoke while you go through the process of stopping. You can get rid of all your doubts and fear first, so when it comes time to extinguish that final cigarette you are already a non-smoker and enjoying being one.

The only chapter that has caused me to question my original advice seriously is this chapter on the matter of the right timing. I advise that if your special cigarette occasions are stress situations at the office, then pick a holiday to make an attempt, and vice versa. In fact, that isn't the easiest way to do it. The easiest way is pick what you feel to be the most *difficult* time to do it. In this way you can prove to yourself right out of the blocks that you can handle even the toughest situations as a non-smoker and the rest becomes even easier. But if I gave you that as a definite instruction, would you even make the attempt to stop?

Let me use an analogy. My wife and I plan to go swimming together. While we arrive at the pool at the same time, we are rarely in the water together. The reason for this is that my wife enters the water extremely slowly, dipping one toe in, then another, and so on. For me, even watching this is excruciating. I know that no matter how cold the water is, eventually I'm going to have to brave it. So I've learned to do it the easy way: I dive straight in. If I were in a position to insist that my wife either did as I did (i.e., dive straight in) or not swim at all, I know that she'd choose not to swim at all. You see the problem.

Feedback from readers tells me that many smokers have used the original advice I gave on timing to delay what they perceive to be the "evil day."

My next thought was to use a technique like the one I used for Chapter 21, *The Advantages of Being a Smoker*. It would be something like, "Timing is very important, and in the next chapter I will advise you about the best time for you to make the attempt." You would turn the page over and there would be a huge "NOW"! That is in fact the best advice, but would you take it?

In a sense, this is the most subtle aspect of the smoking trap. It's designed to hold you for life. When we have genuine stress in our lives, it's not time to stop, and if we have no stress in our lives, we have no desire to stop.

Ask yourself these following questions.

When you smoked that very first cigarette, did you really decide then that you would continue to smoke for the rest of your life?

OF COURSE YOU DIDN'T!

Do you want to be a smoker for the rest of your life?

OF COURSE NOT!

So when will you stop? Tomorrow? Isn't that what you said yesterday? Next year? Isn't that what you said last year?

Isn't this what you've been asking yourself since you first realized you were hooked? Are you hoping that one morning you will wake up and just not want to smoke any longer? Stop kidding yourself. I waited thirty-three years for it to happen to me and never did that day come. With drug addiction you get progressively more hooked, not less. You think it will be easier tomorrow? If you can't do it today, what makes you think you'll be able to tomorrow? Or will you wait until you get one of the killer diseases? Do you honestly think that the additional stress caused by the thought of impending death will make it easier to quit? Think about this. What would you advise your dearest friend to do in this situation? You would urge him to save his life and act immediately.

We believe that we live stressful lives. In fact, we don't. We've taken most of the *genuine* stress out of our lives. We have a comfortable roof over our heads. When we leave our home we aren't likely to be attacked by man-eating predators. Most of us don't have to worry about where our next meal is coming from. We have heat, light and clean water. Compare this to the life of a wild animal. Every time a rabbit comes out of its burrow it is confronted with life-threatening situations. One lapse in concentration and that rabbit could be someone's lunch. But the rabbit is equipped to handle this stress. It has adrenaline and other hormones—and so have we.

The truth is that the most stressful periods in our lives tend to be childhood and early adolescence. The reason for this is that everything is new and everything is changing. But during this most stressful period of our lives, we didn't need to smoke. We were perfectly able to cope because 3.8 billion years of evolution has equipped us to do so.

I was five years old when World War II started. We were bombed out of our home in London and I was separated from my parents for two years. I was billeted with people who treated me unkindly. It was an unpleasant period in my life, but I was able to cope with it. I don't believe it has left me with any permanent scars; on the contrary I think it has made me a stronger person. When I look back on my life there has only been one thing I couldn't handle and that was my slavery to that damned weed.

Twenty-five years ago, I thought I had all the worries in the world. I was suicidal—not in the sense that I wanted to jump off the top of a building but in the sense that I knew my smoking would soon kill me. I argued that if this was life with my crutch, life just wouldn't be worth living without it. What I didn't realize was that when you are physically and mentally depressed, everything gets you down. Today, I feel like a young boy again. Only one thing has made that change in my life: I'm now out of the smoking pit.

I know it's a cliché to say that "if you haven't got your health you haven't got anything" but it's true. I used to think that physical fitness fanatics were a pain. I used to claim that there was more to life than feeling fit: like booze and smokes.

That's nonsense. When you are physically fit you can enjoy the highs more and cope with the lows better. We confuse responsibility with stress. Responsibility becomes stressful only if you are not strong enough to handle it. Characters like Humphrey Bogart, Peter Jennings and George Harrison were strong, dynamic, powerful people. What destroys them is not the stresses of life, or the pressure of being in the public eye, but the so-called crutches they turn to in order to try to handle that stress. Unfortunately these crutches can kill and sadly for those fine men and millions like them, cigarettes did just that.

Look at it this way. You've already decided that you are not going to stay in the trap for the rest of your life. Therefore at some time in your life, whether you find it easy or difficult, you will have to go through the process of getting free. Smoking is not a habit or a pleasure. It is drug addiction and a disease. We've already established that, far from being easier to stop tomorrow, it will get progressively harder. With a disease that's getting progressively worse, the time to get rid of it is NOW—or as near to now as you can practically manage. You are about to trade in a beaten up old pickup truck for a brand new Ferrari. Why wait another day?

Just think how wonderful it will be not to have your life dominated by a four-inch tube of paper with poison in it. Just think how wonderful it will be to replace a life of fear, anxiety, stress and slavery with one of health, happiness and freedom! Why wouldn't it be easy—and fun?

Just follow all my instructions. You won't only find it easy after extinguishing the final cigarette: YOU'LL ENJOY IT!

CHAPTER 29

WILL I MISS THE CIGARETTE?

No! Once that little nicotine "monster" is dead and the chemical addiction is broken, any remaining brainwashing will vanish and you will find that you will be both physically and mentally better equipped not only to cope with the stresses and strains of life but to enjoy the good times to the fullest.

There is only one danger and that is the influence of people who are still smoking. There is a saying that, "The grass is always greener on the other side." Nowhere is this attitude more prevalent than in the area of smoking. Why is it in the case of smoking, where the disadvantages are so enormous and the illusory "advantages" so slight, that ex-smokers tend to envy smokers?

With all of the brainwashing we are exposed to during our childhood and adolescence it is no surprise that we experiment with cigarettes and become hooked. But why is it that as soon as we manage to break free, we immediately once again want to become a smoker? It is the influence of smokers.

It usually happens at a social occasion, maybe on vacation with friends. After a meal, a smoker lights up and the ex-smoker remembers that this is an occasion when previously he would have smoked. He forgets about the many awful disadvantages of smoking and sees the cigarette as something that would help him to really relax after a meal. This momentary sense of deprivation causes a pang. This is a very curious scenario because what the ex-smoker should be remembering is how miserable smoking made him and how the smoker is envying him for being a non-smoker. This is much closer to the truth because, let's face it, every smoker on the planet, even with the warped, addicted, brainwashed mind suffering the delusion that he enjoys smoking, would rather be a non-smoker. So why do some ex-smokers envy smokers on such occasions? There are two reasons.

Just one cigarette. Remember: "just one cigarette" doesn't exist. Stop seeing the cigarette as a single object and see it how it really is: just one more link in the endless chain of smoking. Don't envy smokers; pity them. It helps to observe smokers closely. Notice how agitated and irritable they get when they can't smoke. Notice how quickly they smoke that cigarette, and how quickly they light the next. Notice how they are only happy when they are not aware that they're smoking and how self-conscious and apologetic they are when they are aware of it. Remember: they aren't enjoying any of them; they are merely feeding their addiction. But by feeding the addiction they are ensuring that they'll need to go on feeding it. So long as they feed it, it will never go away.

In particular, remember that after that meal, that social occasion or that vacation, those poor smokers have to smoke all day, every day for the rest of their lives, never being allowed to stop, even for a day. The next morning, when they wake up with a mouth like a cesspit and a throat like sandpaper, what will be the first thing they do? That's right, light a cigarette and start the cycle all over again. That's what smoking is: a life sentence where life means a life of filth, disease, fear, misery and slavery.

The next time those smokers inadvertently see the health warnings, the next time they have a heart flutter or pains in their chest, the next time they're the only smoker in a group of non-smokers, the next time they are going out and feel anxious because they don't know if they'll be able to smoke, those poor smokers will have to continue to pay a fortune for the privilege of poisoning and suffocating themselves to death. And for what? Why do they live this life of slavery and pain? To remove that little empty feeling caused by withdrawing from the previous cigarette, so they can temporarily feel like a non-smoker. This is all smokers are trying to achieve; the state of peace they enjoyed before they ever lit that first cigarette. And what is the only thing preventing them from enjoying that feeling permanently? The cigarette!

The second reason why some ex-smokers (almost always people who have quit using willpower) have pangs on these occasions is because the smoker is doing something (i.e. smoking) and the ex-smoker is not. This can lead to a feeling of deprivation. Get it clear into your mind before you start: it is not non-smokers who are being deprived; it is smokers.

Smokers are deprived of their:

HEALTH
ENERGY
MONEY
SELF-CONFIDENCE
PEACE OF MIND
COURAGE

SELF-ESTEEM
SELF-RESPECT
TRANQUILLITY
FREEDOM

Get out of the habit of envying smokers and start seeing them for the sad, enslaved creatures they really are. I know: I was the world's worst. That is why you are reading this book, and the ones who cannot face up to this reality, who have to go on kidding themselves, are the most pathetic of all.

You wouldn't envy a heroin addict. Opiate use kills around 3,000 Americans a year. Nicotine kills over 450,000 Americans and an estimated five million worldwide. It has already killed far more people on this planet than all the wars in history combined. Like all drug addiction, yours won't get better. Each year it will get worse, just as it has already since the first time you smoked. If you don't enjoy being a smoker today, you'll enjoy it even less tomorrow. Don't envy smokers; pity them. Believe me, THEY NEED YOUR PITY.

CHAPTER 30

WILL I PUT ON WEIGHT?

This is another myth about smoking, spread mainly by people trying to quit using willpower and who substitute food for cigarettes. The withdrawal pangs from nicotine are very similar to hunger pangs, so the two are easily confused and some people might eat when they aren't really hungry. However, whereas eating can relieve a hunger pang, the withdrawal pangs from nicotine can never be satisfied so long as you remain a smoker.

As with any drug, after a while the body builds immunity and the drug ceases to relieve the symptoms that the previous dose created. As soon as we extinguish a cigarette, the nicotine begins to leave the body, so the withdrawal symptoms with their hunger-like pangs return.

The smoker is therefore left with a permanent "hunger" that he can never satisfy. This is why many smokers turn to over-eating, heavy drinking and even harder drugs in order to satisfy this perceived "void." As I mentioned in an earlier chapter, the vast majority of alcoholics are smokers. I wonder if this is really a smoking problem disguised as a drink problem.

For the smoker the natural tendency is to start by substituting nicotine for food. During my own nightmare years I got to the stage where I cut out breakfast and lunch entirely. I would chain-smoke during the day. In the later years I would actually look forward to the evenings because I could stop smoking and give my poor lungs some respite from the punishment. However, I would be picking at food all evening. I thought it was hunger, but it was really withdrawal pangs from nicotine. In other words, during the day I would substitute nicotine for food and during the evenings, food for nicotine.

In those days I was thirty pounds heavier than I am today and there wasn't a thing I could do about it.

When that "little monster" leaves your body the feeling of insecurity leaves with it. Your confidence returns, together with a marvelous feeling of achievement and self-respect. You feel in control of your life, and you can use that control to determine not only your eating habits, but in a wide variety of wonderful ways. This is one of the many great advantages of being free from this awful weed.

As I have said, the weight myth is perpetuated by will-power quitters who substitute food for cigarettes during the withdrawal period, and then continue to overeat. Let's be clear about this: stopping smoking does not lead to weight gain; overeating does. Food and any other substitutes make it harder to quit smoking, not easier, as I shall explain in Chapter 37.

Provided you follow all the instructions, weight gain should not be a problem for you. However, if you already have a weight problem, or you want more information to give you peace of mind, I would recommend that you read *Allen Carr's EASY-WEIGH to Lose Weight* which is based on the same principles as this book and makes weight control a pleasure.

CHAPTER 31

AVOID FALSE
INCENTIVES

Many smokers, while trying to stop by using willpower, try to increase their levels of motivation by providing themselves with false incentives.

There are many examples of this. A typical one is "My family and I can have a great vacation on the money I will save." This appears to be a logical and sensible approach, but in fact it is a false incentive because any smoker would rather smoke fifty-two weeks a year and not have a vacation. In a way, this approach can even heighten the sense of deprivation because the smoker now perceives that he has to abstain for fifty weeks to go on a vacation that he feels that he'll never be able to enjoy without a cigarette anyway. This makes the cigarette even more precious in the smoker's mind. Instead, you should focus on the other side of the equation: What am I getting out of the cigarette? Why do I need to smoke?

Another example: "I'll be able to afford a better car." That's true, and the incentive may help you abstain until you get that car, but what then? Once the novelty has gone you will feel deprived, and sooner or later you will fall for the trap again.

Another typical example is the office or family bet or pact. These sometimes have the advantage of helping to motivate you at certain times of the day, but they almost always end in failure. Why?

1. The incentive is false. Why should we want to stop just because other people are doing so? All this does is to create additional pressure, which increases the sense of deprivation and sacrifice. If you and a group of friends, family or colleagues want to quit together, and plan on supporting each other through the process, that's great. But a pact tends to create additional pressure that can make it difficult for a group member to ask for help if they are struggling. This can turn participants into secret smokers, which increases the sense of deprivation and dependency even further.

2. The "rotten apple" theory, or inter-dependence. With the willpower method of stopping, the smoker is a fragile creature undergoing a period of misery and torture while waiting for the urge to smoke to disappear. For reasons I have already discussed, using this method one or more participants are guaranteed to fail, and this failure will come sooner rather than later. This gives the other participants the excuse they have been waiting for. With the pact broken or the bet won, the other participant(s) have no motivation to stay stopped. It's not their fault—they would have held out—it's just that Bruce or Doug or Sharon let them down. The truth is that most of them have already been cheating themselves.

3. "Sharing the credit" is the flip side of the "rotten apple" theory. It's true that the loss of face is not so bad when shared around, but who wants to fail in the first place? The problem is that if, against all the odds you are using willpower and you do succeed, you have to share the credit with the other members of the group. I'm not one to hog the limelight, but stopping smoking is a truly major event and it's only right and proper that you get all the credit that this wonderful achievement deserves.

Another classic example of a false incentive is the bribe; i.e., the parent offering the teenager money to remain smoke-free or the bet, "I'll give you one hundred dollars if I fail." There was once an example of this in a TV program I was watching. A policeman attempting to quit using willpower put a one hundred dollar note in his cigarette pack. He had a pact with himself. He could smoke again, but before he did so, he had to set light to the one hundred dollar bill. This stopped him for a couple of days, but eventually he burned the note. I wouldn't have lasted twenty minutes.

Stop kidding yourself. If the $150,000 that the average smoker needs to earn to finance his addiction won't stop him, or the one-in-two risk of contracting a life-threatening disease, or the lifetime of mental and physical slavery, then what chance does a one hundred dollar bill—or any other false incentive—have? False incentives make quitting harder, not easier, because they force us to focus on the illusory sacrifice the smoker makes. Keep looking at the other side of the tug of war—the side based on facts, not fear.

What is smoking doing for me? ABSOLUTELY NOTHING.

Why do I need to do it? YOU DON'T! YOU ARE ONLY PUNISHING YOURSELF.

CHAPTER 32

THE EASY WAY TO STOP SMOKING

This chapter contains instructions about the easy way to stop smoking. Providing you follow these instructions, you will find that stopping ranges from relatively easy to enjoyable!

It is ridiculously easy to stop smoking. All you have to do is two things.

1. Make the decision that you are never going to smoke again.
2. Don't mope about it. Rejoice.

You are probably asking, "Why the need for the rest of the book? Why couldn't you have said that in the first place?" The answer is that at some stage you would have moped about it, and consequently doubted your decision. You would have been forced to use willpower and, as a result, most likely would have failed.

As I have said before, the smoking trap is a very subtle and sinister one. The main problem in quitting is not the chemical withdrawal, which is barely even noticeable, but the brainwashing and it was therefore necessary to explode those myths and illusions. Understand your enemy. Know his tactics, and you will easily defeat him.

I spent thirty-three years trying to stop smoking the hard way and suffered seemingly endless weeks of black depression. When I finally broke free I went from a hundred cigarettes a day to zero without a single bad moment or pang of regret. I even enjoyed the withdrawal period because I saw it for what it really was—a barely noticeable feeling in the pit of my stomach, which was a signal that the "little monster" was dying. The truth of the matter is that stopping smoking is the most wonderful thing that has happened in my life.

I couldn't understand why it had been so easy and it took me a long time to work it out. It was this. I knew for certain that I was never going to have to smoke again. During my previous attempts, no matter how determined I was, I was basically *trying* to stop smoking, hoping that if I could survive long enough without a cigarette, the urge would eventually go. Of course it didn't go because I was waiting for something to happen, and the more I moped about it, the more I wanted a cigarette, so the craving never went.

My final attempt was different. Like all smokers nowadays, I had been giving the matter serious thought for some time. Up to then, whenever I failed, I had consoled myself with the thought that it would be easier next time. It never occurred to me that I might have to go on smoking for the rest of my life. This thought filled me with horror and started me thinking very deeply about the subject.

Instead of lighting up subconsciously, I became more aware of my smoking and began to analyze my thoughts and feelings as I was doing it. This confirmed what I already knew.

I wasn't enjoying any of them, and they were truly filthy and disgusting.

I started looking at non-smokers. Until then I had always regarded non-smokers as wishy-washy, humorless, unsociable and pedantic people. However, when I looked more closely it became clear that, if anything, they appeared stronger and far more relaxed than smokers. They seemed to be able to handle stress perfectly well without smoking, and it was obvious that they were having far more fun than smokers. They had energy and a zest for life that I envied.

I started talking to ex-smokers. Up to this point I had regarded ex-smokers as people who had been forced to stop smoking for health reasons or because they could no longer afford it, but that had a secret longing to smoke. A few did say, "You get the odd pang, but it really isn't worth bothering about." But most said: "Miss it? You must be joking. I've never felt better in my life."

Talking to ex-smokers exploded another myth I had always believed. I thought there was some inherent weakness in me, but it suddenly dawned on me that all smokers go through this private nightmare. Basically, I said to myself: "Millions of people are stopping and are much happier now than when they were smokers. I didn't need to do this before I got started and I had to work hard to get used to the filthy things. So why do I need to do it now?" I now knew that I didn't enjoy smoking. In fact I hated the whole filthy business, and I did not want to spend the rest of my life being the slave of this disgusting weed.

I said to myself: "Allen, whether you like it or not, YOU HAVE SMOKED YOUR LAST CIGARETTE."

I knew, right from that point that I would never, ever smoke again. I wasn't expecting it to be easy; in fact, just the reverse. I fully believed that I was in for months of black depression and that I would spend the rest of my life having the occasional pang. Instead it has been absolute bliss right from the start.

It took me a long time to work out why it had been so easy and why I had not suffered those terrifying withdrawal pangs that had plagued all of my previous attempts. The reason is that they only exist in the mind. They are created by doubt and uncertainty. If you remove the doubt, the "cravings" never come.

The beautiful truth is that IT IS EASY TO STOP SMOKING. It is only the indecision and moping about it that makes it difficult. Even when they are addicted to nicotine, smokers can go for relatively long periods without smoking and it doesn't bother them. It is only when you *want* a cigarette but can't have one that the sense of deprivation comes.

Therefore the key to making it easy is to make your decision certain and final. Not to *hope* you have kicked it, but to *know* you have. Never doubt or question your decision. In fact, celebrate it.

If you are able to bring this degree of certainty to this endeavor, it will be easy. But how can you be certain from the start unless you know it is going to be easy? This is why the rest of the book is necessary. There are a couple of essential points and it is necessary to get them clear in your mind before you start.

1. Realize that you can do this. There is nothing different about you that makes quitting uniquely challenging. Millions of Americans have done it, and you can too. The only person who can make you smoke that next cigarette is you.

2. There is absolutely nothing to give up. On the contrary, there are enormous positive gains to be made. I do not only mean you will be healthier and wealthier. I mean that you will be able to enjoy the good times more and that your ability to cope during the bad times will improve.

3. Get it clear in your mind that there is no such thing as one cigarette. Smoking is drug addiction and a chain reaction.

The first cigarette you ever smoked is responsible for every one you have ever smoked.

4. See smoking for what it really is. It is not a sociable habit with some unfortunate side effects. It is drug addiction and a disease. Face up to the fact that, whether you like it or not, YOU HAVE GOT THIS DISEASE. It won't go away just because you bury your head in the sand. Remember: like all progressive diseases, it gets worse and worse. The easiest and best time to rid yourself of this disease is *now*.

5. Separate the disease (i.e., the chemical addiction) from the frame of mind of being a smoker or a non-smoker. All smokers, if given the opportunity to go back to the time before they became hooked, would jump at that opportunity and choose a non-smoking life. You have that opportunity today! Embrace it! Don't even think about it as "giving up" smoking. As soon as you make the decision to smoke your final cigarette you become a non-smoker. You should celebrate right from the outset, and you should continue to celebrate for the rest of your life.

By this stage, if you have opened your mind as I requested at the beginning, you will have already decided you are going to stop. If you have the right frame of mind, your success is guaranteed. Many readers are now feeling excitement at the prospect of their new lives and are straining at the leash to get on with it, barely able to wait to get the poison out of their system.

If you have a feeling of doom and gloom, it will be for one of the following reasons.

1. Something has not quite "clicked" in your mind. Re-read the above five points and ask yourself if you genuinely believe them to be true. If you doubt any point, re-read the appropriate chapter or chapters.

2. You fear failure itself. Do not worry. Just read on. You will succeed. The whole business of smoking is like a confidence trick on a grand scale. Intelligent people do fall for confidence tricks, but only once. Having seen through the smoking illusions, you will not fall for the same con trick again so you should have no fear of failure.

3. You agree with everything, but you are still miserable. Don't be! Open your eyes. Something wonderful is happening. You are about to escape from the prison. Anyway, it is the cigarette that is causing the misery—non-smokers aren't miserable when they can't smoke!

It is essential to start with the correct frame of mind: "Isn't it great that I am a non-smoker!"

All we have to do now is to keep you in that positive frame of mind during the withdrawal period (three days), and the next few chapters deal with specific points that will enable you to do just that. By the end of the withdrawal period you will be thinking this way automatically and naturally as you begin to experience the delights of being a non-smoker. At that stage, the only mystery in your life will be "It is so obvious, why couldn't I see it before?" However, two important warnings:

1. Delay your plan to smoke your last cigarette until you have finished the book.

2. I have mentioned several times a withdrawal period of three days (after which you are 100% nicotine-free). This can cause misunderstanding. First, you may subconsciously feel that you have to suffer for three days. Provided you have the right mindset, which means seeing quitting not as losing a friend, but as killing an enemy, you don't. Secondly, avoid the trap of thinking, "Somehow I have just got to abstain for three days and then I will be free." Nothing will

actually happen after three days. You won't suddenly feel like a non-smoker. Non-smokers do not feel any different from smokers. If you are moping about stopping during the three days, in all probability you will still be moping about it after three weeks, three months or even three years. What I am saying is, if you can start right now by saying, "I am never going to smoke again. Isn't it wonderful?" all temptation will go. Whereas if you say, "If only I can survive three days without a cigarette," you will be dying for a cigarette after the three days are up.

CHAPTER 33

THE WITHDRAWAL PERIOD

Although you are 100% nicotine-free after three days of abstinence it can take up to three weeks before your mind and body become fully accustomed to the absence of nicotine and many of the other thousands of chemicals present in tobacco smoke. It is not uncommon to experience smoking thoughts during this period. These consist of two quite separate factors.

1. The physical withdrawal pangs of nicotine—that slightly empty, insecure feeling, like hunger, which smokers identify as a "need" to smoke.

2. The psychological trigger of certain events such as a telephone conversation or a coffee break.

It is the failure of willpower quitters to understand and differentiate between these two factors that make their attempts

162

to quit so miserable and unsuccessful. Although "pangs" are not painful as such, it is important not to underestimate their potential influence if we approach this task with the wrong mental attitude.

If smokers using willpower to quit can manage to abstain for a few days, the physical component of the "pang" disappears. It is the psychological triggers that cause the difficulty. That smoker has grown accustomed to relieving his need to smoke at certain times of the day and when doing certain things. Over time, these associations can become quite strong. Thus the smoker forms the view that he can't have a coffee, or drink a beer, or take a break, or enjoy a meal without a cigarette. It is important to deal with this point and best to do so by using an example.

Let's say that you buy a brand new car, and true to Murphy's Law, instead of the signal lever being on the left, as with your old car, it is on the right. You know it's on the right, but for a couple of weeks, until you become accustomed to it, you occasionally put the windshield wipers on whenever you want to signal.

Stopping smoking is similar. During the early days of being quit, certain events may trigger the thought, "I want a cigarette." This is because for all of the years you were a smoker, you associated this specific event with smoking. In such situations, "I want a cigarette" becomes a conditioned reflex. It is essential to counter-condition your response in these situations otherwise you will interpret your conditioned "I want a cigarette" response as fact and then feel deprived because you can't have one. This is the beginning of the slippery slope of having to use willpower.

A common such trigger is a meal, particularly one at a restaurant with friends. The ex-smoker having to use willpower already feels depressed and deprived. When his friends light up after the meal this feeling is doubled. Because the brainwashing still exists in his mind, he believes that his friends are enjoying the cigarette rather than merely removing the dissatisfied state of needing to smoke. This compounds the feeling of deprivation further and the ex-smoker needs to use substantial amounts of willpower to get through the occasion. The saddest thing here is that even though he is not smoking, the cigarette is still dominating the ex-smoker's life.

Even with my method, responding correctly to these "triggers" is the most challenging part and it can make the difference between finding stopping an "OK" experience and a wonderful, life-changing one.

It is essential to counter this conditioning from the start and to do so successfully you must replace the fear and confusion caused by the brainwashing with hard facts. Get it clear in your mind: you don't need to smoke and you don't need to torture yourself by regarding the cigarette as some sort of crutch or friend when you know for a fact that it is neither. There is no need to be miserable. Cigarettes don't make meals or social occasions; they ruin them. Smokers aren't smoking after a meal because they enjoy it, but because they are drug addicts who need their "fix" after a period of abstinence.

Abandon the ridiculous concept of smoking as being pleasurable for its own sake. If we smoked just for the sake of smoking, we could smoke herbal cigarettes. (No, not that kind of herb!) The reason that herbal cigarettes haven't taken off here or anywhere else is that there is no point in smoking them because they haven't got any nicotine. We can clarify this point by comparing it with heroin. Do you think a heroin addict shoots up because he enjoys using a hypodermic or to get the drug? It's so obvious with other people's addictions, isn't it? Smokers smoke to get nicotine, not because they enjoy the act of smoking. As a vivid demonstration of this, look at the story of *Next*.

Next was launched by the world's biggest tobacco company, Philip Morris, in 1989. It was touted as a nicotine-free cigarette and the nicotine was removed by using high-pressure carbon dioxide in a process similar to the method used by coffee companies when making decaffeinated coffee (they were referred to as "de-nic" cigarettes internally at Philip Morris). Smokers hated them though. After experimenting with them, it began to dawn on smokers that there is no point in smoking apart from to get the nicotine, and that there was no pleasure in the physical act of smoking for its own sake. The product flopped and was withdrawn.

Once you can see that there is no aspect of smoking that is remotely approaching pleasurable, you will have no more need to stick a cigarette in your mouth than you would in your ear.

Whether the pang is due to physical withdrawal or the psychological trigger mechanism, accept it. There is no physical pain and with the right mental approach you can brush it off as if it were a bit of fluff on your sleeve.

Instead of feeling fearful and anxious about pangs, embrace them. Say to yourself: "I know what this is—it's the "little monster" dying. This is what smokers suffer from their whole lives and that's what keeps them smoking. Non-smokers don't get these pangs. Isn't it great that I am breaking free from this awful addiction and looking forward to a life of freedom?"

Don't focus on the pang, but on what it represents—the death not of a friend, but of a terrible enemy. One that enslaved you for years and stole your health, your money, your self-respect, your courage and confidence, all the time trying to kill you.

Think of the next few days and weeks as a game of poker where you have a Royal Flush and your opponent doesn't even have a pair of twos. You have the better cards and will crush him, so he'll try to cheat and trick you. Whatever he throws at you doesn't matter because it doesn't change the facts. You have the winning hand. You are going to win and at last be able to claim the prize you so richly deserve—a life of health, happiness and freedom.

You have him just where you want him. You have used facts to see through the confusion and fear that he has created to try to keep you trapped. As every minute passes, he becomes weaker. It's over. You have won. You are free.

Whatever you do, don't try *not* to think about smoking. This is a tactic used by people who are quitting using willpower. They try not to think about smoking, but of course this makes them think about it even more. Soon they are obsessed and can't get the cigarette out of their mind. You *will* think about smoking—but it's *what* you are thinking that is important. Whenever you think about smoking, think how wonderful it is that you have broken free. SAVOR EACH THOUGHT AND EACH MOMENT. REMIND YOURSELF HOW WONDERFUL IT IS TO BE FREE ONCE AGAIN AND CELEBRATE THE PURE JOY OF NO LONGER BEING A PRISONER, A SLAVE AND AN ADDICT.

As I have said, with this mental approach, pangs that would torture a willpower quitter will become moments of pure pleasure and achievement for you. You will be amazed at how quickly smoking becomes a total non-issue in your life.

Willpower quitters frequently doubt their decision to quit because they still suffer from the illusion that they enjoyed smoking and this causes the sense of deprivation we have already discussed at some length. You, on the other hand have removed any doubts and as a result can focus on enjoying the process of breaking free and remaining a happy non-smoker.

If one of your smoking friends offers you a cigarette, you can be proud to say, "No thanks," safe in the knowledge that he will be envying not only the fact that you are a non-smoker, but such an obviously happy one. It'll hurt him to think that one more smoker has broken out of the prison, but at the same time it'll give him hope that maybe he too can get free.

Remember that you have traded in a life of fear, misery and slavery for one of health, happiness and freedom. Remember the tens or even hundreds of thousands of dollars that one cigarette would cost you and ask yourself whether you would pay this money just to be a slave to something that you detest and will most likely kill you in the most terrible way imaginable.

Some smokers fear that they will have to go through the rest of their lives reversing these conditioned responses that smokers have in certain situations. In other words, they see themselves as having to use psychological tricks to kid themselves into believing that they don't need to smoke. This is not so. I am not asking you to use mindless optimism to drown out rational thought; I'm asking you to use rational thought to drown out fear and confusion. There is a saying that the optimist sees the bottle as half-full and the pessimist sees it as half-empty. In the case of smoking, the bottle *is* empty and the smoker sees it as full. It is the smoker who has been brainwashed, not the rest of society! Once you start telling yourself that you don't need to smoke, and letting yourself be happy about not having to smoke, it's amazing how quickly this replaces the conditioned response of the brainwashed smoker. The reason that this "takes" so easily is because it is the truth. You do not need to smoke. It's the last thing you need to do; make sure it isn't the last thing you do.

CHAPTER 34

JUST ONE DRAG

This is the undoing of many smokers who try to stop using willpower. They will go through three or four days smoke-free and then have the odd couple of drags, "just to tide them over." They do not realize the devastating effect this has on their frame of mind.

For the vast majority of relapsing smokers, the first drag is disgusting, and this gives them a conscious boost. They think, "Good, it wasn't enjoyable. I'm losing the urge to smoke." The point is that CIGARETTES WERE NEVER ENJOYABLE. Enjoyment wasn't the reason you smoked; if it was, nobody would ever smoke more than one cigarette.

The only reason you smoked was to feed that "little monster" again. You were a drug addict. Just think: you had starved him for three or four days and he was, to all intents and purposes, dead. Then you threw him a lifeline. How precious that one cigarette or puff must have been to him! Now he alive again, craving nicotine. You may not be consciously aware of it, but the fix your body received will be communicated to your subconscious mind and all your sound preparation will be undermined. There will be a little voice at the back of your mind saying, "In spite of all the logic, they *are* precious. I want another one."

That single drag has two damaging effects.

1. It keeps the "little monster" alive in your body, craving nicotine.

2. It keeps the "big monster"—the brainwashing—alive in your mind, wanting a cigarette. If you take a drag, what's to stop you taking another one? Or one hundred, or one million?

Don't play this dangerous game. There is only one loser—you. I absolutely guarantee you that you will be back smoking regularly before you know it. Just one cigarette is exactly how every smoker on the planet started, and it is also how every single ex-smoker on the planet relapsed.

Don't play games with yourself over something this important. If you have one drag, you will be smoking for the rest of your life.

CHAPTER 35

WILL IT BE HARDER
FOR ME?

The combinations of factors that will determine how easy
each individual smoker will find it to quit are infinite. To
start with, each of us has his own character, personal circumstances, motivation, timing, etc.

In my experience, people from certain professions tend to
find it harder than others, because they find it difficult to let go
of the brainwashing.

An example might be work that combines short bursts of
intense, stressful activity with extended periods of inactivity.
Car salesmen for example have a lot of "downtime" when they
are bored and they tend to smoke to provide a distraction. These
long periods of relative inactivity are often followed by or sand-
wiched between periods of intense activity and pressure, when
they smoke for the illusory "relief" it gives them.

Homemakers are sometimes in a similar situation. No one works harder than a homemaker in my experience, but although much of the work can be stressful, it can also be boring. Long periods of monotonous housework are "rewarded" by a cigarette, and the homemaker's day can be mapped out by limited, and therefore precious, opportunities to smoke.

The challenge for these types of smoker is to see through the brainwashing of the cigarette as an all-purpose stress reliever/stimulant/relaxant/reward/comforter/friend and to see it for what it really is: a drug delivery device, much like the heroin addicts hypodermic syringe. This is easy with the right frame of mind. Believe it or not, it is not compulsory to mope around craving cigarettes when these triggers come. Instead, why not use that opportunity to celebrate your freedom and congratulate yourself that you have got rid of this evil monster?

Remember, any smoker, regardless of age, sex, intelligence or profession, can find it easy and enjoyable to stop provided YOU FOLLOW ALL THE INSTRUCTIONS.

CHAPTER 36

THE MAIN REASONS FOR FAILURE

Based on the enormous amount of feedback we have received over the past twenty-five years, there are two main reasons for failure with the Easyway method.

The first is the influence of other smokers. At a weak moment or during a social occasion (most likely involving alcohol) somebody will light up. I have already dealt with this topic at length. Use that moment to remind yourself that there is no such thing as just one cigarette and that the smoker has to go on smoking all day, every day, for the rest of his life, never being allowed to stop. Remember that the smoker envies you, and feel sorry for him. Believe me, he needs your pity. I wouldn't wish the life of a smoker on my worst enemy.

The other main reason for failure is having a bad day. You need to get it clear in your mind before you start that everyone has good and bad days, whether they smoke or not.

The problem with the willpower quitter is that he tends to blame a bad day on the absence of the cigarette. He mopes around feeling deprived and makes a bad day worse. On the other hand the Easyway Method quitter celebrates the fact that, even though today isn't good, he doesn't have the additional stress and misery of being a smoker on top of it.

When you are a smoker you have to block your mind to the many, many downsides of smoking. Smokers never have smoker's coughs, just permanent colds. They never have to freeze outside in the depths of a Midwestern winter; they just "go for a bit of fresh air." As a smoker, if your car breaks down in the middle of nowhere, you light a cigarette. But does this really help deal with the problem? In such a situation, a willpower quitter would mope for a cigarette, as if the cigarette would solve the problem, but why? Smoking a cigarette does precisely nothing to fix your car or improve your predicament, so why do we attribute these magical properties to it?

This moping creates an impossible situation. You are miserable because you can't smoke, and you'll be even more miserable if you do. You know that you have made the right decision, and you have made that decision based on irrefutable facts. Every smoker on the planet would rather be a non-smoker and every non-smoker is glad they don't have to smoke. Never punish yourself by doubting this decision. It is one of the best, if not the very best decision that you have ever made.

You can be happy, not because Allen Carr tells you to be, but because there is so much to be happy about. This is a fact. As with every other area in our lives, *a positive mental approach is essential—always.*

CHAPTER 37

SUBSTITUTES

Substitutes include gum, candy, pills, patches and chocolate. DO NOT USE ANY OF THEM. They make it harder to quit, not easier because they perpetuate the myth that you have given something up and that you need to replace it with something else. That quitting smoking has left a hole in your life that needs to be filled. Smoking *was* the hole in your life. When you get rid of the cigarette, you fill the hole and are once again complete.

Remember these points:

1. Smoking is a disease. You do not need a substitute disease when you quit.

2. You do not need nicotine. It is poison. You don't need a substitute for poison.

3. Remember: cigarettes create the void; they do not fill it. Non-smokers don't have a "void." The quicker you truly

accept that you do not need to smoke, or do anything else in its place, the sooner you will be truly free.

In particular avoid any product that contains nicotine, whether it is gum, patches, nasal sprays, inhalators or the latest and most bizarre gimmick, e-cigarettes. It is true that a small proportion of smokers who attempt to quit using nicotine substitutes do succeed and attribute their success to such use. However I believe that they quit in spite of their use and not because of it. It is unfortunate that many doctors still recommend Nicotine Replacement Therapy (NRT).

The medical community's love affair with NRT is not entirely surprising though. We tend to think that there is a pill for everything these days. Actually, the theory behind NRT sounds reasonable and logical. It is based on the belief that when you quit smoking, you have two powerful enemies to defeat:

1. The psychological or psycho-social triggers which make up the "habitual" side of smoking
2. The terrible physical withdrawal from nicotine

If you have to take on two enemies, common sense would tell you that it is probably better to do it one at a time. So the theory behind NRT is to continue to take nicotine while you fight the psychological side of the addiction. Once this objective is achieved, we can then wean ourselves off the physical side of the addiction. In this way, you are tackling each problem separately.

The problem with this is that it is based on a flawed premise. Smoking isn't a habit: it's drug addiction and the actual physical withdrawal from nicotine is so slight as to be virtually imperceptible.

Furthermore, NRT implies that smokers only go through withdrawal whenever they try to quit. In fact, smokers go through withdrawal throughout their smoking lives, and it is the desire to relieve these feelings of withdrawal that creates the perceived "need" to smoke. As soon as the smoker extinguishes a cigarette, the nicotine begins to leave the body. Even in smokers who metabolize nicotine relatively slowly, within a couple of hours their nicotine levels have dropped to less than half. During those first few hours the smoker is experiencing withdrawal at its worst, which is interesting because every smoker on the planet can (and does) regularly go for hours without smoking and it doesn't bother them in the slightest.

After eight hours just under 3% of the nicotine from that cigarette remains (along with minor residual amounts from previous cigarettes). Even chain-smokers can sleep eight hours at night without waking to smoke. By the morning, in purely physical terms, we are virtually nicotine-free. After just three days, we *are* nicotine free. This begs the question of why we need to use NRT for such extended periods (the patch, for example, is a ten-week program). All this does is prolong the life of the "little monster" and, because your brain associates getting nicotine with cigarettes, it keeps the big monster alive and wanting to smoke.

Think about it this way. Would you tell an alcoholic who was trying to quit to drink beer instead of wine? To stop being a nicotine addict you must stop taking nicotine. All the people we see in our seminars who are addicted to nicotine gum remind me of this simple, unarguable truth. Don't be fooled by the fact that the gum tastes awful—so did the first cigarette, remember?

NRT also has two other important negative impacts on the psychology of the quitter.

1. It convinces the smoker that the physical withdrawal from nicotine is so bad that he needs a patch or gum to handle it. This, because of the power of the mind, becomes a self-fulfilling prophecy. A smoker who could previously

go several hours without a cigarette with no bother at all, suddenly experiences terrible "physical withdrawal" just a few minutes into his quit. How can this possibly have anything to do with nicotine?

2. The use of NRT products (indeed any substitute) also perpetuates the notion that the smoker is "giving something up"—that nicotine does something more than merely remove the symptoms of withdrawal created by the previous dose. This, as I have said repeatedly, leads to a sense of sacrifice, and it is this that triggers feelings of deprivation, misery and vulnerability. This necessitates the use of enormous amounts of willpower, which in turn leads to failure rates in excess of 90%. Real life studies of the patch and gum seem to indicate a twelve-month success rate of around 7%.

   All substitutes have exactly the same effect. I'm now talking about this business of "I can't have a cigarette, so I'll have ordinary chewing gum, or sweets, or peppermints to help fill the void." Although the empty feeling of wanting a cigarette is indistinguishable from hunger for food, one will not satisfy the other. In fact, if anything is designed to make you want a cigarette, it's stuffing yourself with chewing gum or peppermints.

The launch of Zyban is one of the biggest and most controversial changes to the smoking cessation landscape in recent years. It has been around as an anti-depressant (Wellbutrin) for quite a while, but was repackaged as a cessation aid in the late 1990s.

I quit many years before it was launched, but I have read extensively about Zyban and spoken to hundreds of smokers who have attempted to quit by using it. I have to admit to being fairly bemused by the whole concept of it. In addition to admitting "it is unclear exactly how Zyban works" which I find a little alarming, the manufacturer's website states that Zyban "reduces the urge to smoke." But what is an "urge," and how do you measure it? How can you scientifically measure two different "urges" from two different people? An "urge" isn't something uniform that you can measure like a sack of potatoes; every single one is different and every person is different. Anyway, why try to "reduce the urge to smoke" when it's just as easy to remove it altogether?

Think of two Zyban quitters sitting having coffee together. One says, "Wow! That was a huge craving. This Zyban isn't working." The other says, "I had one too. But mine was OK. This Zyban is really working!" Might it be possible that these two people had the identical feeling but that due to a million outside factors, they interpreted and processed those feelings differently? Could it be possible that one person has a lower discomfort threshold?

Isn't this all really saying that the desire to smoke is mental, and that we can use the power of the mind to reduce or even eliminate the desire to smoke? This is the EASYWAY—to remove the desire to smoke. Why do we need a drug to help us do this? Why not just use an open mind and facts? Why not permanently remove our desire at a cognitive level, rather than merely temporarily suppressing it? If we are not confronting and dealing with our desire to smoke, but merely using a drug to suppress it, what happens when you stop taking the medication? Does the desire to smoke return?

Interestingly, both Zyban and NRT manufacturers advocate fairly intensive counseling as a critical element of their respective programs; in fact, it is difficult to find published success rates for these products without the counseling element, which makes it difficult to evaluate their true efficacy.

For me, there is something counter-intuitive about treating drug addiction with drugs (particularly the drug you are trying to kick). Zyban only began to make sense to me after a conversation I had with a doctor from Vancouver who attended a seminar. He said that he prescribed Zyban to willpower quitters "to cope with the symptoms of depression caused by quitting using willpower." This makes perfect sense to me: he is prescribing it as an anti-depressant, which is precisely what it is.

Using the EASYWAY, you don't need an anti-depressant, because there is nothing to be depressed about. On the contrary, this can and should be one of the most enjoyable experiences of your life.

The latest quit smoking "wonder drug" is Chantix. The varenicline molecule contained in Chantix sits on receptor cells in the brain, blocking nicotine from acting on those cells and in theory preventing smoking from removing the slightly anxious, edgy feeling of withdrawal. Pfizer's five initial trials of Chantix showed an average twelve-month success rate of 22%, but it should be noted that these rates were achieved under highly artificial clinic study conditions. How much of that 22% success rate was due to the 26% one-on-one counseling sessions provided to study participants? How many real-world Chantix quitters would have such a luxury? In addition, ever since it was launched, Chantix has been associated with brutal side effects including suicidal thoughts, depression and anxiety. The smokers we see in our seminars instinctively back away from taking such heavy medication, and rightly so, in my view.

But the chief downside of substitutes is that they prolong the real problem, which is the brainwashing. When you recover from a bad dose of the "flu," do you look for a replacement disease? Of course you don't. By saying "I need a substitute for smoking" you are really saying "I am making a sacrifice by quitting." This is the cause of the depression and misery experienced by both smokers (throughout their smoking lives whenever they are in a situation when they can't smoke) and people quitting using willpower. All substitutes do is substitute one problem for another. There is no pleasure in stuffing candy down your throat. You will just get fat and miserable, and in no time at all, you'll find yourself back on the weed, but this time twenty pounds heavier.

Casual smokers find it difficult to dismiss the belief that they are being deprived of their little reward or crutch: the cigarette during the coffee break at work or the smoke break while working in a dull or high-pressure job. Some say, "I wouldn't even take the break if I didn't smoke." This proves my point. Often, the break is taken not because we want or need it, but so we can feed the "little monster." Those smokers aren't enjoying the cigarette though; just the ending to the feeling of needing it. By removing that feeling, they get to feel temporarily like a non-smoker. These cigarettes are the equivalent of wearing tight shoes to get the pleasure of taking them off.

So if you absolutely feel that you must have your little reward then wear a pair of tight shoes and don't take them off until you go on a break. Then you can experience the reward of relaxation and satisfaction of taking them off. Perhaps you would feel rather stupid doing this. You would be right to. However, this is pretty much what smokers do all day every day. Soon you will see this whole aspect of the "reward" for what it really is—just another occasion when smokers have to go on feeding the "little monster."

If you are in a profession where you really need a break—homemakers, doctors, teachers etc., then you'll soon be enjoying that break ten times more because you can use it to really relax, not to have to ingest a battery of poisons and other harmful chemicals. More importantly you can choose to take the break when you really want it rather than when your addiction obliges you to.

Remember, you don't need a substitute. Every pang, however minor, is a symptom of recovery and you will be fully recovered before you know it. Let that knowledge be your reward. Enjoy ridding your body of this poison, and your mind of the slavery and dependence.

I have covered the topic of weight gain in Chapter 30, but weight and substitutes are so closely linked that I feel the need to reiterate the points that I have already made:

1. A nicotine pang can feel like a mild hunger pang. So if you find yourself getting "hungry" at odd times of the day, it's more likely to be a nicotine pang. Just brush it off and celebrate yet another sign of your recovery.

2. Nicotine speeds up the metabolism slightly but its effect on your weight when you stop smoking is minimal. Nicotine also robs you of energy and once you stop smoking increased energy levels cause many people to actually lose weight on this method because instead of moping around eating chocolate and feeling deprived, you feel like getting out and doing things with all of your new-found energy and confidence.

In my experience the stories we hear about people putting twenty, thirty or forty pounds on are always due to substituting food for cigarettes. You won't feel the need to substitute with this method so you shouldn't have any issues caused by substitution.

If there were any truth about cigarettes and weight control you would never see an overweight smoker, and there are plenty of those around; I should know, for years I was one.

In the US, the constitutional right to free speech is one of the most cherished. If cigarettes really relieved stress, controlled weight, helped us relax and concentrate etc., tobacco companies would claim it on the pack. The fact that none of these claims appear on the pack is proof that they are not true. In fairness, it is smokers, not tobacco companies, who make these claims. As a senior tobacco executive said in 1982, "We should start to see ourselves as a drug company rather than a tobacco company."

If you put on a couple of pounds over the next couple of weeks, don't worry. After years of punishment due to smoking, it takes our bodies a little while to settle back down. As I have said repeatedly; stopping smoking doesn't make you put weight on, overeating does. Be sensible, don't substitute, eat properly, exercise and you will be feeling—and looking—like a million dollars before you know it.

CHAPTER 38

SHOULD I AVOID
TEMPTATION?

Up until now, I have been categorical in all my advice and would ask you to treat this advice as instruction rather than suggestion. The reason for this is twofold: first, because there are sound, practical reasons for my advice and, second, because those reasons have been backed up by the experience of hundreds of thousands of successful EASYWAY quitters.

On the question of whether or not to try to avoid people or situations you associate with smoking during the early days of your quit, I regret that I cannot be categorical. Each smoker will need to decide for himself. I can, however, make what I hope will be helpful suggestions.

Every smoker fears that when they stop smoking they also have to stop living. I am delighted to tell you that the opposite is true—with the cigarette out of your life, you can really start living. This fear is really just a fear of the unknown and it is this that keeps us smoking year after year. This fear consists of two distinct phases.

1. *How can I survive without a cigarette?* This is the same fear that smokers get when they are out late at night and running low on cigarettes. Of course it's caused by the cigarette. Non-smokers never feel this fear. Indeed, one of the sweetest things about becoming a non-smoker is to be free from the constant, nagging fear.

   This fear is purely psychological and thoroughly irrational. Think about it rationally. Why should we have a fear of not poisoning ourselves to death? The question should not be "How can I survive without the cigarette?" but "How did I survive being a smoker all these years?" It's amazing our bodies can put up with the punishment. Life without cigarettes is normal, natural and fun—look at the millions of non-smokers and ex-smokers who are getting through life quite happily without the burden of drug addiction and the slavery of smoking. They've done it and so can you. It's only smokers who obsess about cigarettes and get panicky when they can't smoke. Non-smokers couldn't care less. And neither will you once you have made the decision to break free and take your life back.

2. *Will life ever be the same without the cigarette?* This tends to be a longer-term fear. That once you are through the initial period and life becomes normal, you will be left with a void. I'm delighted to tell you that life without cigarettes is dramatically better than life as a smoker and that you will feel the benefits for the rest of your life. True, life does settle back down as you become accustomed to your freedom, energy, improved health and surplus cash, but it settles at a level way above that that a smoker has to endure. It may help to make some detailed notes about your life

as a smoker. These notes can be used in the future to refer back to. Remembering how miserable life was as a smoker will help you to stay happy about getting, and staying, free. Sometimes, to appreciate our freedom, we have to remember what it was like to be a slave.

As I said, there are situations that you associate with smoking and you need to develop a strategy for dealing with them. Let's look at a couple of scenarios.

1. *I'll keep a pack of cigarettes close by, just in case.* The failure rate among people that do this is several times higher than those that don't so my advice is to remove all smoking materials from your house, car, office etc. The reason for this is simple. By having cigarettes on or close to your person, you are sub-consciously positioning the cigarette as the "solution" if you have a problem. Try to see it the way it really is. The cigarette *is* the problem, not the solution. Would you recommend that an alcoholic trying to quit drinking keep a bottle of scotch handy? Does a non-heroin addict carry a fix around with him "just in case"? Shortly, you will be a non-smoker, and non-smokers don't need cigarettes.

   The worst thing about this tactic is that it creates doubt in your mind. We want to remove doubt, not create it! If you still feel the need to have cigarettes with you then I suggest you re-read this book from the beginning because something hasn't "clicked." However I believe the main reason for the higher failure rate in these cases is that the smoker does not feel completely committed to stopping in the first place. Remember the two essentials to success are:

   1) Certainty that you are doing the right thing by stopping and 2) a positive mindset: "Isn't it great that I don't need to smoke?"

2. *Should I avoid stressful or social occasions?* By all means, try to avoid stressful situations (who needs them?) but don't be frightened if they do materialize. As a non-smoker you will be far better able to handle stress because you will be happier and healthier. You also won't be suffering the constant stress of being a drug addict.

As for social occasions, my view is that you have achieved something wonderful and that you should celebrate from square one, not sit at home moping. Remember—you haven't lost a friend; you've killed a deadly enemy. This enemy was not only trying to kill you, but was also stealing from you; your health, energy, self-confidence and self-esteem, money and your freedom. Why wouldn't you be happy to get rid of such an evil monster? "Get out and enjoy yourself!" is my advice. There is so much to be happy about and the sooner you get out and have fun, the sooner you receive affirmation of the wonderful decision you have made to break free.

CHAPTER 39

THE MOMENT OF REVELATION

The moment of revelation usually takes place about three weeks after a smoker stops. The sky appears to become brighter and as the last of the poison is swept away, the last of the brainwashing disappears along with it. Instead of telling yourself you do not need to smoke, you suddenly realize that the last thread is broken and you can enjoy the rest of your life without ever needing to smoke again. It is also usually from this point that you start looking at smokers as worthy of pity.

Smokers using willpower rarely experience this wonderful moment because, although they are glad to be non-smokers, they never truly understand that there was nothing to "give up" and they continue to feel deprived.

The more you smoked, the more enjoyable this moment is, and the feeling lasts a lifetime.

I consider myself to have been very fortunate in this life and have had some truly wonderful moments; but the most wonderful of all was the moment of revelation. With all of the other highlights in my life I can remember how happy I was but cannot recapture the actual feeling. I just cannot get over the joy of not having to smoke any more. If ever I am feeling low and need a boost, I just think how lovely it is not to be hooked on that awful weed. Nearly all of the letters I receive from people who have broken free the EASYWAY echo this sentiment—that quitting smoking was the best thing they ever did. Ah! What pleasure you have to come!

With over twenty years of feedback from the seminars and the book, I have learned that most people experience the moment of revelation within days, not weeks as stated above.

In my own case, it happened even before I put out my final cigarette. This is relatively common at our seminars; a smoker will say something like, "You don't have to say another word, Allen. I can see everything so clearly, I know I'll never smoke again." Over the years I have learned to tell when it happens without the individual even saying anything, and it is a thrilling moment and a privilege to be a witness to it. From the letters I receive I'm also aware that it frequently happens with the book.

Ideally if you follow all the instructions and understand the psychology completely, it should happen to you over the next couple of days.

Nowadays at the seminar I tell smokers that the physical withdrawal period is around three days and that after three weeks you are truly free, but I dislike giving these kinds of guidelines. It can cause two problems. Firstly it creates an expectation that the smoker will have to suffer for three days or three weeks. As I have already stated, this is not so; with the right frame of mind the whole process is enjoyable right from the beginning. The second is that it creates an expectation that at the end of the third week something earth shattering will happen. As an example, it is possible that someone finds the first three weeks easy but that during the fourth, he experiences one of those dreadful days we all occasionally have, whether we're a smoker or a non-smoker. This might knock his confidence.

You might reasonably say, "Don't give any guidelines then." The problem with this is that with no expectation of what to expect, the ex-smoker is left in limbo, waiting for nothing to happen.

What is the significance of three days and three weeks? These timescales are not carved in stone but are based on the many years of feedback I've received. After three days the nicotine has left your body (as I have stated, most of it actually leaves in the first couple of hours) and you are technically no longer an addict. It's often around this time when the ex-smoker ceases to be pre-occupied with smoking. What usually happens is that you are in a stressful or social situation that previously you were unable to get through without smoking, and you realize that it didn't even occur to you to light up. From this point on it's usually plain sailing—don't get complacent though!

Three weeks is usually around the time when people feel that they have really broken free. This is also usually the time when most serious attempts to quit with willpower fail. Willpower quitters sense around this time that they have lost the desire to smoke and so they let their guard down. They smoke a cigarette to show themselves that they're in control and of course, get immediately re-addicted. They try not to capitulate immediately, but they are on the slippery slope back to smoking full-time.

The key to the problem is not to wait for the moment of revelation but to realize that you have total control over this process and that it is up to you to decide how you want this whole experience to play out. If you are miserable and depressed, guess what will happen? If you are happy and excited about your new life of health, happiness and freedom, guess what will happen?

The instant you extinguish your final cigarette, it's over. You've won. No force on earth can prevent you from claiming the life that you have earned and the life you deserve. Go out, be proud, savor this moment and embrace your future free from the slavery of drug addiction.

CHAPTER 40

THE FINAL CIGARETTE

Having decided on your timing, you are now ready to smoke that last cigarette. Before you do so, check on the two essentials:

1. Do you feel certain of success?
2. Do you have a feeling of doom and gloom or a sense of excitement and anticipation that you are about to achieve something really wonderful?

If you have any doubts, re-read the book first. If you still have doubts, contact your nearest Allen Carr's Easyway center, details of which are listed at the back of this book. One of our facilitators will be happy to discuss any comments or questions you might have.

Remember, you never decided to fall into the smoking trap. But that trap is designed to enslave you for life. In order to escape you need to make the positive decision that this will be your final cigarette and that you will never again force yourself to do something that makes you feel so awful.

Remember, the only reason you have read this book so far is because you would dearly love to escape. So make that positive decision now. Make a solemn vow to yourself that when you extinguish that final cigarette, come what may, you will never smoke another.

Perhaps you are concerned that you have made vows like this several times in the past but are still smoking, or that you will have to go through some awful trauma. Have no fear, the worst thing that can possibly happen is that you fail, and so you have absolutely nothing to lose and so much to gain.

But stop even thinking about failure. The beautiful truth is that it is not only ridiculously easy to quit but also extremely enjoyable. Instead, why not focus on the wonderful gifts you are about to receive as a non-smoker? Health, life, happiness, freedom…the list is endless!

Why make it hard on yourself? Why not choose the EASY-WAY! All you need to do is follow the simple instructions I'm about to give you:

1. Make the solemn vow now and mean it.

2. Smoke that final cigarette consciously, inhale the filth deeply into your lungs and ask yourself where the pleasure is.

3. When you put it out, do so not with a feeling of: "I must never smoke another," or "I'm not allowed to smoke another," but with the feeling: "Isn't it great! I'm free! I'm no longer the slave of nicotine! I don't ever have to put these filthy things in my mouth again."

4. Be aware that for the next few days, the "little monster" will be inside you looking to be fed. At times I refer to it as a slight physical craving for nicotine. Strictly speaking, this is incorrect, and it is important you understand why. Because it takes time for the "little monster" to die, some ex-smokers assume that it is necessary to suffer cravings during this period. You will be glad to know that this is not the case. The body cannot crave nicotine. Only the brain can crave. Physical withdrawal creates a slight physical feeling a bit like hunger that up to now your brain has interpreted as "I want a cigarette." You need to replace this "conditioned response" with a new one, based on the facts. So when that slight feeling comes, respond by saying to yourself, "YIPPEE, I'M A NON-SMOKER!" and focus on all of the wonderful gifts you are giving yourself by breaking free from the slavery of smoking. Brush that feeling off as if it were a bit of fluff that had somehow landed on your sleeve. In this way, you can be happy about your decision to become a non-smoker, and you can stay happy for the rest of your life. At this time, you can also reflect on the fact that cigarettes only ever brought misery, stress, fear and slavery to your life, and that every smoker on the planet would rather be a non-smoker.

5. Willpower quitters do not recondition their "I want a cigarette" response and therefore continue to crave cigarettes. Because they want to smoke but can't, the feeling of sacrifice and deprivation grows. This requires the use of willpower, which in turn leads to the feelings of panic, anxiety and stress that so many smokers who use the willpower method experience. No wonder they feel so miserable. They spend the rest of their lives desperately moping for something that they hope they will never have. No wonder so few of them succeed and the few that do never feel completely free.

6. It is the doubt and the waiting for nothing to happen that makes it difficult to quit. So never doubt your decision, you know it's the correct one. We could go through the pros and cons of smoking and a thousand times out of a thousand we would choose to be a non-smoker. Having made what you know to be the right decision, don't doubt it. If you do, you will put yourself in a no-win situation. You will be miserable if you crave a cigarette but don't have one and even more miserable if you do smoke it. So why bother? What would it do for you? Many people believe that the difference between smokers and non-smokers is the cigarette. This is only part of the story. The real difference is that non-smokers have *no desire* to smoke. With no desire to smoke, it takes no willpower not to do so. With no desire to smoke, there are no cravings. Why would you crave something you don't want? This is completely within your power to achieve. As soon as you make the decision, you become a non-smoker. If you are happy about your decision, you will become a happy non-smoker.

So, you need to make the decision once and for all, get 100% behind it, and go with it. Be clear in your mind that you only have two choices: you can go through the rest of your life having to smoke all day, every day, never being able to stop, living a life based on fear, misery, disease, addiction and slavery. Or you can break free, take control of your life back and build a future based on health, happiness and freedom from the slavery of smoking. The choice couldn't be easier. This isn't difficult. This is the easiest, and best, decision you'll ever make. Why not let yourself be happy! You deserve it!

YOU ARE ALREADY A HAPPY NON-SMOKER!

And you will remain a happy non-smoker provided:

1. You never doubt your decision.

2. You don't wait to become a non-smoker. You've already won! You are free!

3. You don't try not to think about smoking. Think about it as much as you want and every time, celebrate that you have broken free. "YIPPEE—I'm a non-smoker!"

4. You don't use substitutes. Who needs a substitute for the biggest cause of preventable death in the world?

5. You see all other smokers for the drug addicts they are. Don't envy drug addicts. The truth is that they'll be envying you!

6. Whether they are good days or bad, you don't change your life just because you've recovered from the disease called nicotine addiction. Having recovered, you can now really start living! As the days go by and your health, both physical and mental improves, the highs will appear higher and the lows less low than when you were a smoker.

7. Whenever you think about smoking during the next few days or the rest of your life, think: YIPPEE, I'M A NON-SMOKER!

CHAPTER 41

A FINAL WARNING

No smoker, given the chance of going back in time to before they started smoking, would choose to become one again. Many of the smokers who consult me are convinced that if I could help them to stop, they would never dream of relapsing, yet a small percentage of them do fall for the same trap again.

I trust that this book will help you to find it easy to stop smoking. But be warned: smokers who find it easy to stop can sometimes be prone to relapse, because they think it will be easy to quit again.

DO NOT FALL INTO THIS TRAP?

No matter how long you have been a non-smoker or how confident you are that you could never get hooked; if you smoke again you will instantly become re-addicted.

Make it a rule of life that you don't smoke tobacco. No exceptions. Ever. Period. This is not a game. There are some things in life that you don't mess around with, and this is one of them.

If you do light a cigarette at some time in the future, what would it do for you? You would lose all of the wonderful gifts of health, happiness and freedom you have earned, and for what? So you can return to a life of fear, misery and slavery? By making the decision to break free from smoking, you have just won life's lottery. The prize is life, happiness, health and freedom. Money cannot buy these gifts. Protect them with your life.

CHAPTER 42

OVER TWENTY
YEARS OF FEEDBACK

Since the original publication of this book over twenty years ago, I have been lucky to receive an enormous amount of feedback.

Originally it was a struggle: in the early days the majority of the major players in the tobacco control establishment were critical of my method (most of them without taking the trouble to look at it in detail, I'm sad to say). Over the years, as they have seen the success of the method with their own eyes, this attitude is beginning to change and today some of our most enthusiastic supporters are frontline medical professionals who themselves work with smokers. Throughout Europe, where both the book and the seminars enjoy great success and a wonderful reputation, EASYWAY is considered by many in the field to be the most effective quitting technique available.

As I write this, we are in the process of reaching out to the tobacco control community and building and expanding our network of centers in the US so that smokers across North America can also have access to the EASYWAY method.

The EASYWAY program is also now available over the internet so that smokers who do not have access to a seminar center can attend a seminar in webcast form.

I'm no do-gooder. My war—which, I emphasize, is not against smokers but against the nicotine trap—I wage for the purely selfish reason that I enjoy it. Every time I hear of a smoker escaping from the prison I get a feeling of great pleasure, even when it has nothing to do with me. You can imagine the immense pleasure I obtain from the tens of thousands of grateful letters and emails that I have received over the years.

There has also been considerable frustration. The frustration is caused mainly by two categories of smoker. First, in spite of the warning contained in the previous chapter, I am disturbed by the number of smokers who find it easy to stop, yet get hooked again and find they can't succeed the next time. This applies not only to readers of the book but also to a few attendees at our seminars.

A man phoned me a few years ago. He was distraught; in fact, he was crying. He said, "I'll pay you $2,500 if you can help me stop for a week. I know if I can just survive for a week, I'll be able to do it." I told him that I charged a fixed fee and that was all he need pay. He attended a group session and, much to his surprise, found it easy to stop. He sent me a very nice thank you letter.

The very last thing we say to ex-smokers leaving our seminars is: "Remember, you must never smoke another cigarette." This particular man said, "Have no fear, Allen. I'll definitely never smoke again."

I could tell that the warning hadn't really registered. I said, "I know you feel like that at the moment, but how will you feel six months on?"

He said, "Allen, I will never smoke again."

About a year later there was another phone call. "Allen, I had a small cigar at Christmas, and now I'm back on forty cigarettes a day."

I said, "Do you remember when you first phoned? You hated it so much you were going to pay me $2,500 if you could stop for a week. Do you remember you promised you would never smoke again?"

"I know. I'm a fool."

It's like finding someone up to his neck in quicksand and about to go under. You pull him out. He is grateful to you then, six months later, dives straight back in.

I admit to feeling sad, angry and frustrated at such smokers, but this quickly turns to sympathy when I realize that they are feeling ten times worse than I. If you find yourself in this situation you need to accept responsibility for your actions, give yourself an almighty kick in the pants and focus on how to clean up the mess.

If re-reading this book does not help, contact our US office at 1 866 666 4299. And do it quickly.

Ironically, one of the problems with my method is that some people find it too easy. This makes them lose their fear of smoking because they figure that they can smoke when they want and find it easy to quit again. EASYWAY doesn't work that way. It is easy to stop smoking, but it's impossible to control it.

Just one cigarette led to the years of addiction and slavery you had to suffer. And just one cigarette will do it again. Do you really want to be a smoker for the rest of your life? Haven't you already decided that this is the *last* thing you want? The only essential to being a non-smoker is not to smoke.

The other category of smoker that causes me frustration is those smokers who are too frightened to even try or, when they do, sabotage themselves at every turn and therefore find it a great struggle. The main difficulties appear to be the following:

1. **Fear of failure**. The point is that as a smoker, you are already a failure. You therefore have absolutely nothing to lose and potentially a tremendous amount to gain.

2. **Fear of the panic feeling and of being miserable**. These fears are caused by the cigarette. Non-smokers don't have them.

   One of the sweetest things about not having to smoke is to be free of these fears. If you do begin to feel uncomfortable, slow your breathing down and take a couple of nice, big, deep breaths. Focus on the key thoughts: there is nothing to "give up" apart from a life of fear, misery and slavery; every smoker is envious of you as a non-smoker, because every smoker would rather be a non-smoker; that the little monster is dead or already dying. If you go back to smoking you are guaranteeing a future of feeling panicky and miserable. Is that how you want to go through the rest of your life? No one can stop time. Every second that passes, the fear recedes. Enjoy your inevitable victory. If you want to shout, scream or cry then do so. These are all perfectly natural ways to relieve tension. Remember— you are not feeling this way because you stopped smoking, but because you started in the first place. You cannot and will not fail because your life and your future depend on your success.

3. **Not following the instructions.** Incredibly, some smokers say to me, "Your method just didn't work for me." They then go on to describe how they ignored not only one instruction but practically all of them. (For clarity I will summarize these in a checklist at the end of the chapter.)

4. **Misunderstanding instructions.** These occasional mis-understandings appear to be based around the following:

a. *I can't stop thinking about smoking.* Of course you can't, and if you try, you will create a phobia and be miserable about it. It's like trying to fall asleep at night: the more you try, the harder it becomes. It is inevitable that you will think about smoking. It's *what* you are thinking that's important. If you are thinking, "Oh, I'd love a cigarette," or "When will I be free?" you'll have to use willpower not to smoke, which will likely make you feel miserable. But if you are thinking, "YIPPEE! I am free!" you'll be happy, and the more you think about it, the happier you'll be.

b. *When will the "little monster" die?* As I have mentioned, nicotine leaves your body very rapidly. You may continue to feel that empty, insecure feeling because many things cause it, including hunger, stress or fear—none of which are necessarily related to smoking. Incidentally, this is why so many willpower quitters are never quite sure that they've kicked it and never feel truly free. They incorrectly interpret a normal hunger pang or slightly nervous feeling about, say, making a big presentation at work, as a nicotine pang. In any case, the feeling is so slight that most people don't even know it's there.

c. *Waiting for the moment of revelation.* As the saying goes: a watched pot never boils. Don't sit around waiting for it. Get out and enjoy your life and it will come.

I once stopped for three weeks using willpower. I met an old school friend and ex-smoker. He said, "How are you getting on?"

I said, "I've survived three weeks."

He said, "What do you mean, you've "survived" three weeks?"

I said, "I've gone three weeks without a cigarette."

He said, "What are you going to do? "Survive" for the rest of your life? What are you waiting for? You've done it. You're a non-smoker."

I thought, "He's absolutely right. What am I waiting for?" Unfortunately, because I didn't fully understand the nature of the trap at that time, I was soon back in it, but the point was noted. You become a non-smoker when you extinguish your last cigarette. The important thing is to be a happy non-smoker from the start.

d. *I am still craving cigarettes.* How can you claim, "I want to be a non-smoker," and then say, "I want a cigarette"? That's a contradiction. If you say, "I want a cigarette," you are saying, "I want to be a smoker." Non-smokers don't want to smoke cigarettes. These thoughts imply a continued desire to smoke. Re-read this book to identify the problem area or contact our US office on 1 866 666 4299.

e. *I've opted out of life.* Why? All you have done is stop choking yourself. You don't have to stop living. You have just saved your life, not lost it! Over the next couple of days, you will be experiencing a very mild sensation. This sensation is so mild that most people aren't even aware of it. When you were a smoker, you experienced this sensation—a slightly empty, insecure feeling—pretty much throughout your smoking life: when you slept, when you were working, when you went to the movies etc. It didn't bother you when you were a smoker, so why let it bother you now? It didn't stop you trying to lead a full life then, so why should it do so now? Life is for living, so go enjoy it. If there are smokers present, so what? Remember, you are not the one being deprived; they are. Smokers are deprived of their health, their money, their self-respect, their energy, their self-esteem and their freedom. And for what do they make these incredible sacrifices? So they can remove that little empty, insecure feeling and temporarily feel like a non-smoker! Does this sound like a good deal to you? The truth is that every single one of them will be envying you. Be proud of this wonderful achievement. Enjoy your time in the spotlight! When those smokers see you so happy they'll think you're Superman. And, in truth, you'll feel a bit like him!

f. *I am miserable and irritable.* This is most likely because you haven't fully understood or followed my instructions. Find out which one it is and address it by re-reading the relevant chapter(s) in this book. Some people understand and believe everything I say but still start off with a feeling of doom and gloom, as if something terrible were happening. Of course, the truth is that something wonderful has happened. The terrible thing was when you became a smoker, and the terror continued throughout all those years of slavery. If health, happiness and freedom aren't enough for you, then you have bigger problems than smoking. Why be miserable and make it hard on yourself when the reality is that you have so much to celebrate?

The Checklist

If you follow these simple instructions, you cannot fail.

1. **Make a solemn vow that you will never, ever, smoke, chew, suck or otherwise consume anything that contains nicotine, and stick to that vow.**

2. Get this clear in your mind: **there is absolutely nothing to give up.** By that I don't mean that you will be better off

as a non-smoker (you've known that your entire smoking life); nor do I mean that the pleasure or benefit from smoking is not worth the expense and risk. What I mean is that there is absolutely no benefit to smoking whatsoever. It is like banging your head against a wall because it feels a bit better when you stop.

3. **There is no such thing as** a confirmed smoker. You are just one of the millions who fell for this subtle trap. Like millions of ex-smokers who once thought they couldn't escape, you have escaped.

4. If you were to weigh up the pros and cons of smoking, the conclusion would always be the same—to be a non-smoker and happy about it. **Having made what you know to be the correct decision, don't ever make yourself miserable by doubting it.**

5. **Don't try not to think about smoking** or worry that you are thinking about it too much. But whenever you do think about it—whether it's today, tomorrow or the rest of your life—think, "YIPPEE! I'M A NON-SMOKER!"

6. **DO NOT use any form of substitute.**

7. **DO NOT carry or keep any smoking materials.**

8. **DO NOT avoid other smokers.**

9. **DO NOT change your lifestyle in any way purely because you've stopped smoking.**

   If you follow the above instructions, you will soon experience the moment of revelation. But:

10. **Don't wait for that moment to come.** Just get on with your life. Enjoy the highs and cope with the lows. The moment will come, and when it does, it's a moment of pure joy.

CHAPTER 43

HELP THE SMOKER
LEFT ON THE
SINKING SHIP

Smokers are panicking these days. There has been a huge change in society. Not too long ago, you could smoke anywhere; today smokers are shoved outside into the freezing cold. Even smokers regard smoking as antisocial. They sense that the whole thing is coming to an end, and they are right. Every year, millions of smokers are quitting and smokers left in the trap are acutely aware of this.

Every time a smoker successfully escapes from the sinking ship, the ones left on it feel more miserable and more threatened. Every smoker instinctively knows that it is ridiculous to spend a fortune for rolled up dried vegetable matter, to set light to it and to breathe the cancerous fumes into your lungs. So smokers blatantly lie about their "habit," not only to others, but also to themselves. They have to. This is essential if they are to retain some self-respect. They feel the need to justify what they know in their hearts to be unjustifiable behavior. They buy into the brainwashing because they have no other option; and they vigorously defend their smoking as a "right" or a "personal choice." But this is really just putting lipstick on a pig because to admit the truth would leave them feeling frightened.

If a smoker tries to stop by using willpower, he feels deprived and miserable. All this does is to confirm to other smokers how right they are to keep smoking.

Non-smokers don't feel the need to justify their decision to be non-smokers. Some decisions are such no-brainers that they do not need explanation or justification. Smokers therefore don't really understand that it is easy and fun to be a non-smoker. Instead, they believe that becoming one will involve making a tremendous sacrifice. This intimidates the smoker and contributes to the fear that keeps him smoking.

As a non-smoker you can help smokers to see that it is easy and fun to be a non-smoker. Show the smoker that there is nothing to fear, nothing to "give up" and absolutely everything to gain. Tell him how wonderful it is not to have to choke yourself, how lovely it is to wake up feeling fit and strong and to be able to really breathe. Tell him how great it feels to be free of the terrible, unremitting, unrewarding slavery of smoking. Tell him how it feels to finally be free of the conflict and stress of being a smoker. Even better, get him to read this book.

It is essential not to belittle the smoker by muttering away about second-hand smoke or ostentatiously waving away the smoke and pretending that it's choking you to death. Remember how much you hated such people when you were a smoker? Please don't turn into one of them, for goodness sake. Ex-smokers already have a bad reputation with smokers. This reputation is entirely due to the influence of ex-smokers who have quit by using willpower. Part of that ex-smoker still believes that he made a sacrifice when he quit. He continues to feel somewhat vulnerable and copes with this vulnerability by attacking the smoker. This might make him feel better, but it does absolutely nothing for the smoker, apart from to confirm that all ex-smokers are miserable, sanctimonious do-gooders with nothing better to do than to tell others how to run their lives. I had no time for such people when I was a smoker, and I have no time for them now. In this situation, the ex-smoker's attack causes the smoker to feel anxiety, frustration and fear. These add up to stress, and what's the first thing a smoker wants to do in a stress situation? That's right—light up.

Although the change in society's attitude to smoking is the main reason why so many want to quit, it doesn't make it easier for them to do so. In fact, it makes it a great deal harder. Today in the US every smoker who leaves his or her house is subjected to severe restrictions on where and therefore when he or she can smoke. The restrictions are so severe that the smoker becomes obsessed with planning the next opportunity to smoke. This has the effect of making every cigarette seem precious, and this of course feeds the illusion that there is some pleasure in smoking. The reality is that all the smoker is "enjoying" is removing the feeling of deprivation and temporarily feeling like a non-smoker.

These periods of enforced abstinence don't even substantially reduce the amount a smoker smokes; they just mean that the smoker chain-smokes during the few occasions he or she can smoke unhindered. The smoker is "loading up" because they don't know when their next opportunity will come around.

The tighter the smoking restrictions and the more profound the disdain society displays towards smokers, the more the smoker has to change his lifestyle to revolve around the cigarette and the more ostracized he feels.

Society has made the mistake of demonizing the victim instead of the disease. Out of the many tragedies that surround the subject of smoking, surely this is one of the most tragic.

It's strange that even though heroin addicts are technically criminals in law, our instinct as a community is to try to help them in any way we can. Let us adopt the same attitude with smokers. Smoking isn't a choice; it's an addiction. The smoker smokes because he doesn't think he can stop. The smoker endures year after exhausting year of addiction and mental and physical slavery. We always say that a quick death is better than a slow one, so do not envy the poor smoker. He deserves to be treated with sensitivity, respect and dignity. And he also deserves your pity.

CHAPTER 44

ADVICE TO NON-SMOKERS

Help Get Your Smoking Friends or Relatives to Read This Book

First study the contents of this book yourself and try to put yourself in the place of the smoker.

Do not attempt to force him to read this book or try to stop him smoking by telling him that he is ruining his health or wasting his money. He already knows this better than you do. Smokers do not smoke because they enjoy it or because they want to. They say this to themselves and others in order to retain some degree of self-respect. They smoke because they feel utterly dependent on cigarettes, because they think that the cigarette helps them relax and cope with stress and because they sense that life will never be enjoyable without smoking. If you try to force a smoker into quitting, this will make him want to smoke more. This makes each cigarette appear precious which in turn makes it harder to quit.

Instead, concentrate on the other side of the coin. Get him into the company of ex-smokers (there are more than sixty million of them in the US). It will do him good to realize that there are millions of people who have been through this exact same experience. When I was a smoker it never occurred to me that all smokers felt the way I did; and that all ex-smokers had felt like this before they quit. Once he sees that there is life after quitting smoking, and that a smoke-free life is infinitely better than the half-life that smokers live, maybe he'll begin to feel a little less intimidated by the prospect of escaping.

Once you have him believing that maybe he can stop, his mind will start to open. Suggest that it seems obvious non-smokers aren't missing out on anything, and that it looks to you like smokers don't enjoy smoking, but that they smoke to remove the need to smoke.

For many smokers, this observation—so obvious to non-smokers—comes as a bolt from the blue. At this stage, he is ready to start reading this book. He'll be expecting to plough through reams of statistics and technical data about lung cancer and heart disease. Tell him that this book was written by a former chain-smoker and that a grand total of nine pages of this book talk about anything related to health. Keep pointing out that it's only a book and that there is no pressure to quit—if he wants to keep smoking afterwards then he can. Tell him that one of the instructions in the book is to keep smoking—that will get his interest!

Help During the Early Days of a Quit

Whether a recent quitter is suffering or not, assume that he is. Do not try to minimize his suffering by telling him how easy it is to quit. This will merely irritate him and earn you a filthy look.

Instead, tell him how proud you are, how much better he looks and smells, how much easier he is breathing and point out that his smoker's cough has disappeared. Keep this praise and support going. I cannot even begin to explain how important this is.

Because he is not talking about smoking, you might think he's forgotten about it. He hasn't. Don't avoid talking about it, unless you are asked to do so.

Go out of your way to relieve him of additional stresses and pressures during the early days of his quit. Try to think of ways to make life more interesting and fun. If you want to pamper him and treat him like royalty for a while, I'm fairly sure that he won't complain.

Be aware that if the newly launched ex-smoker has a bad day, he is likely to blame it on having quit smoking. When I was trying to quit using willpower I used to throw a tantrum in the hope that my wife or friends would say, "I can't bear to see you suffering like this. For goodness' sake, have a cigarette." This would thrill me because it gave me an excuse to smoke without losing face. I wasn't "giving in"; I was being instructed to smoke. If the ex-smoker uses this ploy, under no circumstances fall for it. Instead say, "If that's what cigarettes do to you, thank goodness you'll soon be free. How wonderful it is that you had the courage and intelligence to stop."

CHAPTER 45

FINALE: HELP END THIS SCANDAL

In my opinion, cigarette smoking is the biggest scandal in our society. The hypocrisy is incredible. We get uptight about glue sniffing and heroin addiction, but it is smoking that is decimating our society, and it has been doing so for decades. In the US alone, smoking kills an estimated 450,000 people every year, making it easily the biggest cause of preventable death. It is estimated that over thirty million Americans alive today will die from smoking related causes.

State and federal government is by far the biggest beneficiary of tobacco sales in the US. The most recent figures indicate that government makes over $25 billion every year. This dwarfs even the profit that the tobacco companies make, or their $12.6 billion marketing and promotional budget.

Compare this huge sum with the less than $500 million spent on tobacco control every year. This equates to less than

2% of the tax revenue generated by the sale of tobacco products. And of that miniscule $500 million, a negligible sum is spent on helping smokers quit.

The government's annual investment in tobacco control amounts to around ten dollars per smoker per year and just over $1,000 per smoking related death. A comparable calculation for the annual cost of the "War on Drugs" reveals spending of $54 billion. This equates to a staggering $27,000 per head for the estimated two million users of illicit drugs excluding cannabis, or a staggering $908,000 per death.

There is the application of double standards here. We throw resources at heroin addicts—who are technically criminals—giving them treatment, shelter, safe injection sites and subsidized drugs or substitutes; yet the smoker—addicted through no fault of his own to a legal product—is left to suffer with little or no support and to pay a truly exorbitant price—most of which goes to the government—to get his drug.

Doctors, who have been tasked with sticking a band-aid over this gaping wound are overworked and poorly trained in cessation techniques. More often than not, the best a doctor can do is to say a few encouraging words and give you a prescription for a pill or patch that likely contains the drug you are trying to break free from.

In the meantime, incidence of smoking in movies, particularly in movies aimed at teenagers, has never been higher. We have legislation to make it illegal to purchase cigarettes below a certain age, but no law prohibiting possession. Schools are powerless to implement no-smoking rules, apart from in areas where smoking is banned by state or local legislation. Up until 2003 we allowed tobacco companies to continue to sponsor key sporting and cultural events and to promote their brand to impressionable children along the way. We are virtually guaranteeing that our kids will see smoking as cool, desirable and rebellious rather than sad, disgusting and depressing. In their tens of thousands, they are falling into the same trap we fell into, for the same reasons. I really cannot believe that we are standing by and letting this happen.

It is bad enough that smoking has decimated my father's, my own and, most likely, the next generation. Are we going to impose this dreadful burden onto yet another generation? Have we learned nothing?

I just don't understand it. If a salmonella or mad cow outbreak results in a single death we all but call a state of emergency; but here we have a disease which kills around 1,300 Americans a day (and has done for years), yet all we seem to be able to do is tax it.

It has often been said that tobacco is the only legal product that if used precisely as the manufacturer intended, kills you. How many more billions of dollars will we give tobacco companies by way of tax breaks to make products that, sadly, work too effectively? How many more innocent people are we going to let die from this terrible disease? And how many more are we going to allow to become infected with the disease in the first place?

I won't wish you luck—you don't need it. Just follow the instructions contained on the following page. Once you have broken free yourself, please spread the word. I really welcome comments and letters from readers so please feel free to contact us via our network of centers.

I wish you every success and all the best for a healthy and happy future free from the slavery of smoking.

Sincerely,
Allen Carr

FINAL INSTRUCTIONS

You can now enjoy the rest of your life as a happy non-smoker. In order to make sure that you do, you need to follow these simple instructions:

1. Keep this book safely in a place where you can easily refer to it. Do not lose it, lend it out or give it away. It's no bad thing to pick it up occasionally and read a couple of pages. It'll keep you "in the zone." This is your shortcut to attaining the right frame of mind about smoking. Keep it close at hand, in case you need it. Rather than lend it out (trust me—you'll never get it back) gift copies to any friends who show an interest in it.

2. If you ever find yourself envying a smoker, realize that they will be envious of you. You are not being deprived. They are.

3. Remember you did not enjoy being a smoker. That's why you stopped. You do enjoy being a non-smoker.

4. Remember, there is no such thing as just one cigarette.

5. Never doubt your decision never to smoke again. You know it's the correct decision.

6. If you have any difficulties contact your nearest Allen Carr's EASYWAY center. You will find a list of these on the following pages.

Tell Allen Carr's Easyway You Stopped Smoking

Now at last you can say

"YIPPEE! I'M A NON-SMOKER"

You have achieved something really marvelous.

Please share your success with us. Sign the following, add your comments and send it to:

Allen Carr USA, Suite 706, 1133 W Broadway, NY, NY 10010 or email us the same information to: info@TheEasywayToStopSmoking.com

YIPPEE! I'M A NON-SMOKER

Signed:_____ Date:_____

Name:_____

Address:_____

_____

_____

_____ Zip:_____

Email address:_____

Comments:_____

_____

_____

_____

ABOUT THE AUTHOR

The common thread running through Allen Carr's work is the removal of fear. Indeed, his genius lies in eliminating the phobias and anxieties which prevent people from being able to enjoy life to the full, as his bestselling books *Allen Carr's Easy Way to Stop Smoking, The Only Way to Stop Smoking Permanently, Allen Carr's Easyweigh to Lose Weight, Allen Carr's Easyway to Control Alcohol, How to Stop Your Child Smoking,* and *The Easy Way to Enjoy Flying,* vividly demonstrate.

A successful accountant, Allen Carr's hundred-cigarettes-a-day addiction was driving him to despair until, in 1983, after countless failed attempts to quit, he finally discovered what the world had been waiting for: an Easy Way to Stop Smoking. Together with Robin Hayley, whom he appointed as managing director of Allen Carr's Easyway Worldwide, he went on to build a global publishing program and a network of centers that span the globe and have a phenomenal reputation for success in helping smokers quit.

His books have been published in thirty-six different languages in over fifty different countries and DVD, audio, CD-ROM, video game and webcast versions of his method are also available. Allen also nominated Robin as his successor and gave him responsibility for his lasting legacy.

Hundreds of thousands of people have attended Allen Carr's Easyway clinics where, with the highest success rate in the quit smoking industry, they guarantee that you will find it easy to quit smoking or your money back. A full list of centers appears in the back of this book. Should you require any assistance, please do not hesitate to contact your nearest center.

Weight-control and alcohol sessions are now offered at a selection of these centers. A full corporate service is also available enabling companies to implement stop smoking programs in the workplace simply and effectively.

All correspondence and enquiries about Allen Carr's EASYWAY books, DVDs, audios, CD-ROMs, video games and webcasts should be addressed to the London Head Office and Clinic listed at the back of this book.

TESTIMONIALS

"I started smoking when I was twelve, and I tried quitting with almost every method. I used the gum, patches, I even tried using an anti-depressant called Zyban. When I was 25 a friend gave me the book, unfortunately they had not read it and they re-gifted it to me thinking I might read it. I did and I have been a non-smoker since, it has been close to two years and I have no desire for a cigarette ever. In fact the thought of smoking repels me and the smell is barely tolerable. I swear by the book and have since bought copies for friends, recommended it to every smoker I know, and everyone that I know has read it has been successful in quitting."

N. Mallet

"I was a smoker for 34 years. I smoked one pack a day, every day!!! I've tried different methods (medication, patch and the gum) to stop smoking, but nothing worked until I read the book "The Easy Way to Stop Smoking". The book was recommended to me by a co-worker. It's incredible, I've been smoke-free for 8 months now and it's been the longest that I ever been without smoking. Thank you, Mr. Carr for giving me my life/freedom back!!!!"

James Rozoff

"It's been over 12 days and I'm going strong. I've replaced killing myself with living. Thanks to Bertrand who recommended the book to me after quitting himself. Today is day 40 for me and breathing easier walking 3 miles a day and loving life."

Rob Wimmer

"Thanks to your book I was able to quit smoking four-and-a-half years ago. My quality of life has been so much better. The book was so well done. Mr. Carr did a great job. I have found it so easy to stay a non-smoker. Using his methods to not only achieve quitting, but to remain so. Thank you."

Angela Jones

"I am a 69-year-old male who has been smoking for 55 years. Many times attempting to stop but it never worked. Someone directed my attention to your book. I bought it at Amazon.com, started reading it in 2 sessions and when I finished I stopped smoking "Cold Turkey". It was mainly because your book recognized smoking as an addiction which I had never seen it that way.

I am now smoke-free for over a month and I am convinced that I am from now on a Non-Smoker. Thanks for your assistance with my stopping smoking."

Robert van Oeveren

"My acupuncturist told me about Allen Carr's book because she was having trouble taking care of other problems I had. I really did not want to quit—I loved smoking. Also I had this huge fear of going through the agony of trying to quit because I had failed so many times before and thought I had tried everything. However, I trusted my acupuncturist, so I decided to try one last time with Allen's book. I had a terrible attitude about my chances of success and the whole way through the book I was saying to myself, "How can reading a book make you quit smoking?" But, miracle of miracles... It did! I followed his instructions to the letter and at the end of the book I was a non smoker. I had just two days of getting the nicotine out of my system and then I was over it all. There was no agony, no cravings, no overeating—nothing. That was almost 4 years ago. Since then, I have been able to afford life insurance so I can leave something to my daughter—it's not affordable if you're a smoker. I have no problem being around people who do smoke and have never had any desire to start smoking again. By the way, if you have any mistrust of these testimonials, just read the totally unbiased ones on Amazon. com and you will see that they all say the same thing. Allen Carr was a true genius. Thank you from the bottom of my heart!"

Nancy Saltz

"Hi. Last week was my one-year anniversary of being smoke-free. That's a year without a drag, without a puff, nothing. And I'm so amazed. A year and a half ago, if you had told me that I could quit easily, I would have laughed (bitterly, cynically). I mean, I was a HARDCORE smoker. I liked smoking. A lot of my self-image was tied up with smoking. I smoked an easy two packs a day. I should say that this year has been easily the most difficult of my life. My mother died, and I am still dealing with extremely debilitating grief. I had to deal with her complicated estate on my own—no siblings, and she wasn't married—and then, three days after her memorial service, my father went into the hospital, and essentially descended into dementia that lasted for about six months. And there, too, I was the only point-person. So, hideous year. But you know what? I haven't picked up a cigarette. And I can only think that if I can get through a year like this without smoking, I can get through anything. So I'm a non-smoker. An amazed, incredulous, incredibly grateful non-smoker. Thank you."

Maggie Topkis

"Thank you. I wish that I could thank Mr. Carr. Like Mr. Carr, I was a thirty-year nicotine addict. I escaped on Thursday, May 27, 2010, at about 4:00 pm. Most of the credit for this miracle belongs to Allen Carr's little magic book, *The Easy Way to Stop Smoking*. If you are a nicotine addict, you have not read this book enough times and have not followed all of Mr. Carr's instructions. The instructions say "Do not stop smoking while you are reading the book." The book is small. Every sentence and every word are your lifeline. None of the instructions are for your own interpretation or experimentation. Do what it says. It is Easy! God Bless this organization and Allen Carr."

John Dulaney

"I smoked for 34 years, read the book over a 3-day period (smoked during the reading) then finished my last smoke on 6-2-08 @ 6:35 pm. Just like the book said, I really forget that

I used to smoke! I have tried all other options and have made countless attempts but failed every time until I read *Allen Carr's Easy Way to Stop Smoking.* I am 46 years old and I feel so much better! Thank you just isn't enough!"

Anita Grimes

"I was the biggest skeptic—and procrastinator. Until now. I was inspired from a chain-smoking friend who had seemingly quit without any withdrawal symptoms whatsoever. I bought the book and quit immediately after finishing it. That was 9 months ago. My only regret is that I wasted 20 years of my life smoking! I feel fantastic and recommend this program to anyone who will listen. Thank you!"

Kevin Browne

"After a lifetime of smoking, I have been smoke free for almost eight months. I never thought I would be able to quit, but after watching the webcast and reading the book, I smoked my last cigarette. I am truly free and I have never been happier. Thank you for, literally, saving my life. I am forever grateful to Allen Carr and all of you who made it possible for me to find my way. I know in my heart that I will never smoke again. This is my life and I am finally in control. There is no better way to quit. Believe me, I know, I've tried it all. Thank you."

Bernadine Favereau

"After smoking for 10 years, a pack a day, I read Allen's book. And the way I see it, IT SAVED MY LIFE! I have a son now, and I am happy to be here for him, as a non-smoker.

I smoked my last one when I finished the book one and a half years ago. And now that I am free from the prison, I know that I will never smoke again. Thank you Allen and thank you everyone that passes the message by. I can count people who absolutely needed to exist in this world with one hand, and Allen is worth two fingers."

Mario Popoca

ALLEN CARR'S EASYWAY CENTERS

The following list indicates the countries where Allen Carr's Easyway To Stop Smoking centers are currently operational. Check www.allencarr.com for latest additions to this list.

Selected centers also offer sessions that deal with alcohol, other drugs and weight issues. Please check with your nearest center, listed below, for details.

Allen Carr's Easyway guarantee that you will find it easy to stop smoking at the seminar or your money back.

Allen Carr's Easyway-Worldwide Head Office

Park House, 14 Pepys Road,
Raynes Park, London SW20 8NH
Tel: +44 (0)20 8944 7761
Fax: +44 (0)20 8944 8619
Email: mail@allencarr.com
Website: www.allencarr.com

Worldwide Press Office
Contact: John Dicey
Tel: +44 (0)7970 88 44
Email: jd@allencarr.com

USA

Central information and bookings:
    Toll free: 1 866 666 4299
    New York: 212- 330 9194
Email:
    info@theeasyway
    tostopsmoking.com
Website: www.allencarr.com
Seminars held regularly in New York, Los Angeles,Denver and Houston. Corporate programs available throughout the USA.
Mailing address:
    576 Fifth Ave, Suite #903
    New York, NY 10036

CANADA

Central information and bookings:
    Toll free: +1-866 666 4299
    +1 905 849 773
Email: info@theeasyway
    tostopsmoking.com
Website: www.allencarr.com
Seminars held regularly in Toronto, Vancouver and Montreal. Corporate programs available throughout Canada
Mailing address:
    P.O Box 61051
    511 Maple Grove Drive
    Oakville, ON, L6J 6X0

English Therapist:
    Damian O'Hara
French Therapist:
        Rejean Belanger

UK CLINICS

Aylesbury
Tel: 0800 0197 017
Therapists: Kim Bennett,
    Emma Hudson
Email:
    kim@easywaybucks.co.uk
Website: www.allencarr.com

Belfast
Tel: 0845 094 3244
Therapist: Tara Evers-Cheung
Email: tara@easywayni.com
Website: www.allencarr.com

Birmingham
Tel & Fax:
    +44 (0)121 423 1227
Therapists: John Dicey,
    Colleen Dwyer, Crispin Hay,
    Rob Fielding
Email: info@allencarr.com
Website: www.allencarr.com

Bournemouth
Tel: 0800 028 7257
Therapists: John Dicey,
    Colleen Dwyer,
    Emma Hudson
Email: info@allencarr.com
Website: www.allencarr.com

Brighton
Tel: 0800 028 7257
Therapists: John Dicey,
    Colleen Dwyer,
    Emma Hudson
Email: info@allencarr.com
Website: www.allencarr.com

Bristol
Tel: +44 (0)117 950 1441
Therapist:
    Charles Holdsworth Hunt
Email: stopsmoking
    @easywaybristol.co.uk
Website: www.allencarr.com

Cambridge
Tel: 0800 0197 017
Therapists: Kim Bennett,
    Emma Hudson
Email:
    kim@easywaybucks.co.uk
    Website: www.allencarr.com

Cardiff
Tel: +44 (0)117 950 1441
Therapist:
    Charles Holdsworth Hunt
Email: stopsmoking
    @easywaybristol.co.uk
Website: www.allencarr.com

Coventry
Tel: 0800 321 3007
Therapist: Rob Fielding
Email:
    info@easywaycoventry.co.uk
Website: www.allencarr.com

Crewe
Tel: +44 (0)1270 664176
Therapist:
    Debbie Brewer-West
Email: debbie@easyway
    2stopsmoking.co.uk
Website: www.allencarr.com

Cumbria
Tel: 0800 077 6187
Therapist: Mark Keen
Email: mark@easyway
    cumbria.co.uk
Website: www.allencarr.com

Derby
Tel: +44 (0)1270 664176
Therapists:
    Debbie Brewer-West
Email: debbie@easyway
    2stopsmoking.co.uk
Website: www.allencarr.com

Exeter
Tel: +44 (0)117 950 1441
Therapist:
    Charles Holdsworth Hunt
Email: stopsmoking
    @easywayexeter.co.uk
Website: www.allencarr.com

Guernsey
Tel: 0800 077 6187
Therapist: Mark Keen
Email: mark@easyway
    lancashire.co.uk
Website: www.allencarr.com

High Wycombe

Tel: 0800 0197 017
Therapists: Kim Bennett,
    Emma Hudson
Email:
    kim@easywaybucks.co.uk
Website: www.allencarr.com

Isle of Man

Tel: 0800 077 6187
Therapist: Mark Keen
Email: mark@easyway
    lancashire.co.uk
Website: www.allencarr.com

Jersey

Tel: 0800 077 6187
Therapist: Mark Keen
Email: mark@easyway
    lancashire.co.uk
Website: www.allencarr.com

Kent

Tel: 0800 028 7257
Therapists: John Dicey,
    Colleen Dwyer,
    Emma Hudson
Email: info@allencarr.com
Website: www.allencarr.com

Lancashire

Tel: 0800 077 6187
Therapist: Mark Keen
Email: mark@easyway
    lancashire.co.uk
Website: www.allencarr.com

Leeds

Tel: 0800 804 6796
Therapist: Rob Groves
Email: info@easyway
    yorkshire.co.uk
Website: www.allencarr.com

Leicester

Tel: 0800 321 3007
Therapist: Rob Fielding
Email: info@easyway
    leicester.co.uk
Website: www.allencarr.com

Liverpool

Tel: 0800 077 6187
Therapist: Mark Keen
Email: mark@easyway
    liverpool.co.uk
Website: www.allencarr.com

Manchester

Tel: 0800 804 6796
Therapist: Rob Groves
Email: info@easyway
    manchester.co.uk
Website: www.allencarr.com

Manchester

Opening 2013/14
Allen Carr's Easyway To Stop
Drinking Alcohol

Milton Keynes

Tel: 0800 0197 017
Therapists: Kim Bennett,
    Emma Hudson

Email:
  kim@easywaybucks.co.uk
Website: www.allencarr.com

Newcastle/North East
Tel: 0800 077 6187
Therapist: Mark Keen
Email: info@easyway
  northeast.co.uk
Website: www.allencarr.com

Nottingham
Tel: +44 (0)1270 664176
Therapist:
  Debbie Brewer-West
Email: debbie@easyway
  2stopsmoking.co.uk
Website: www.allencarr.com

Oxford
Tel: 0800 0197 017
Therapists: Kim Bennett,
  Emma Hudson
Email: kim@easyway
  bucks.co.uk
Website: www.allencarr.com

Reading
Tel: 0800 028 7257
Therapists: John Dicey,
  Colleen Dwyer,
  Emma Hudson
Email: info@allencarr.com
Website: www.allencarr.com

SCOTLAND

Glasgow and Edinburgh
Tel: +44 (0)131 449 7858
Therapists: Paul Melvin
  and Jim McCreadie
Email: info@easyway
  scotland.co.uk
Website: www.allencarr.com

Sheffield
Tel: 0800 804 6796
Therapist: Rob Groves
Email: info@easyway
  yorkshire.co.uk
Website: www.allencarr.com

Shrewsbury
Tel: +44 (0)1270 664176
Therapist:
  Debbie Brewer-West
Email: debbie@easyway
  2stopsmoking.co.uk
Website: www.allencarr.com

Southampton
Tel: 0800 028 7257
Therapists: John Dicey,
  Colleen Dwyer,
  Emma Hudson
Email: info@allencarr.com
Website: www.allencarr.com

Southport
Tel: 0800 077 6187
Therapist: Mark Keen
Email: mark@easyway
  lancashire.co.uk
Website: www.allencarr.com

Staines/Heathrow
Tel: 0800 028 7257
Therapists: John Dicey,
   Colleen Dwyer,
   Emma Hudson
Email: info@allencarr.com
Website: www.allencarr.com

Surrey
Park House
14 Pepys Road, Raynes Park,
London SW20 8NH
   Tel: +44 (0)20 8944 7761
   Fax: +44 (0)20 8944 8619
Therapists: John Dicey,
   Colleen Dwyer, Crispin Hay,
   Emma Hudson,
   Rob Fielding
Email: mail@allencarr.com
Website: www.allencarr.com

Stevenage
Tel: 0800 0197 017
Therapists: Kim Bennett,
   Emma Hudson
Email: kim@easyway
   bucks.co.uk
Website: www.allencarr.com

Stoke
Tel: +44 (0)1270 664176
Therapist: Debbie Brewer-West
Email: debbie@easyway
   2stopsmoking.co.uk
Website: www.allencarr.com

Swindon
Tel: +44 (0)117 950 1441

Therapist:
   Charles Holdsworth Hunt
Email: stopsmoking@easyway
   bristol.co.uk
Website: www.allencarr.com

Telford
Tel: +44 (0)1270 664176
Therapist: Debbie Brewer-West
Email: debbie@easyway
   2stopsmoking.co.uk
Website: www.allencarr.com

WORLDWIDE CLINICS

REPUBLIC OF IRELAND

Dublin and Cork
Lo-Call (From ROI)
   1 890 ESYWAY (37 99 29)
Tel: +353 (0)1 499 9010
   (4 lines)
Therapists: Brenda Sweeney
   and Team
Email: info@allencarr.ie
Website: www.allencarr.com

AUSTRALIA

North Queensland
Tel: 1300 85 11 75
Therapist: Tara Pickard-Clark
Email: qld@allencarr.com.au
Website: www.allencarr.com

Northern Territory-Darwin
Tel: 1300 55 78 01

Therapist: Dianne Fisher
Email: wa@allencarr.com.au
Website: www.allencarr.com

Sydney, New South Wales
Tel & Fax: 1300 78 51 80
Therapist: Natalie Clays
Email: nsw@allencarr.com.au
Website: www.allencarr.com

South Australia
Tel: 1300 523 129
Therapist: Jaime Reed
Email:sa@allencarr.au
Website: www.allencarr.com

South Queensland
Tel: 1300 85 58 06
Therapist: Tara Pickard-Clark
Email: qld@allencarr.com.au
Website: www.allencarr.com

Victoria, Tasmania, A.C.T.
Tel: +61 (0)3 9894 8866
  or 1300 790 565
Therapist: Gail Morris
Email: info@allencarr.com.au
Website: www.allencarr.com

Western Australia
Tel: 1300 55 78 01
Therapist: Dianne Fisher
Email: wa@allencarr.com.au
Website: www.allencarr.com

AUSTRIA
Sessions held throughout Austria
Freephone: 0800RAUCHEN
  (0800 7282436)

Tel: +43 (0)3512 44755
Therapists: Erich Kellermann
  and Team
Email: info@allen-carr.at
Website: www.allencarr.com

BELGIUM:ANTWERP
Tel: +32 (0)3 281 6255
Fax: +32 (0)3 744 0608
Therapist: Dirk Nielandt
Email: easyway
  @dirknielandt.be
Website: www.allencarr.com

BRAZIL

São Paolo
Therapists - Alberto Steinberg
  & Lilian Brunstein
Email: contato
  @easywaysp.com.br
Tel Lilian
  (55) (11) 99456-0153
Tel Alberto
  (55) (11) 99325-6514
Website: www.allencarr.com

BULGARIA
Tel: 0800 14104
  +359 899 88 99 07
Therapist:
  Rumyana Kostadinova
Email: rk@nepushaveche.com
Website: www.allencarr.com

CANADA

Toll free:
  +1-866 666 4299
  +1 905 849 7736
English Therapist:
  Damian O'Hara
French Therapist:
  Rejean Belanger
Regular seminars held in
Toronto, Vancouver and
Montreal. Corporate programs
available throughout Canada.
Email: info@theeasyway
  tostopsmoking.com
Website: www.allencarr.com

CHILE

Tel: +56 2 4744587
Therapist: Claudia Sarmiento
Email: contacto@allencarr.cl
Website: www.allencarr.com

COLOMBIA
SOUTH AMERICA

Therapist:
  Felipe Sanint Echeverri
Tel: +57 3158681043
E-mail: felipesanint
  @allencarrcolombia.com
Website: www.allencarr.com

CYPRUS

Tel: +357 77 77 78 30

Therapist:
  Kyriacos Michaelides
Email: info@allencarr.com.cy
Website: www.allencarr.com

DENMARK

*Sessions held throughout
Denmark*
Tel: +45 70267711
Therapist: Mette Fonss
Email: mette@easyway.dk
Website: www.allencarr.com

ECUADOR

Tel & Fax: +593 (0)2 2820 920
Therapist: Ingrid Wittich
Email: toisan@pi.pro.ec
Website: www.allencarr.com

ESTONIA

Tel: +372 733 0044
Therapist: Henry Jakobson
Email: info@allencarr.ee
Website: www.allencarr.com

FINLAND

Tel: +358-(0)45 3544099
Therapist: Janne Ström
Email: info@allencarr.fi
Website: www.allencarr.com

FRANCE

Sessions held throughout France
Freephone: 0800 FUMEUR
Tel: +33 (4) 91 33 54 55

Therapists: Erick Serre
and Team
Email: info@allencarr.fr
Website: www.allencarr.com

GERMANY

Sessions held throughout
Germany
Freephone: 08000RAUCHEN
(0800 07282436)
Tel: +49 (0) 8031 90190-0
Therapists: Erich Kellermann
and Team
Email: info@allen-carr.de
Website: www.allencarr.com

GREECE

Sessions held throughout Greece
Tel: +30 210 5224087
Therapist: Panos Tzouras
Email: panos@allencarr.gr
Website: www.allencarr.com

GUATEMALA

Opening 2013
Therapist: Michelle Binford
Website: www.allencarr.com

HONG KONG

Email: info@easyway
hongkong.com
Website: www.allencarr.com

HUNGARY

Seminars in Budapest and 12
other cities accross Hungary
Tel: 06 80 624 426
(Freephone)
or +36 20 580 9244
Therapist: Gabor Szasz
and Gyorgy Domjan
Email: szasz.gabor
@allencarr.hu
Web: www.allencarr.com

ICELAND

Reykjavik
Tel: +354 588 7060
Therapist: Petur Einarsson
Email: easyway@easyway.is
Website: www.allencarr.com

INDIA

Bangalore & Chennai
Tel: +91 (0)80 41603838
Therapist: Suresh Shottam
Email: info@easyway
tostopsmoking.co.in
Website: www.allencarr.com

ISRAEL

Sessions held throughout Israel
Tel: +972 (0)3 6212525
Therapists: Ramy Romanovsky,
Orit Rozen, Kinneret Triffon
Email: info@allencarr.co.il
Website: www.allencarr.com

ITALY
Sessions held throughout Italy
Tel/Fax: +39 (0)2 7060 2438
Therapists: Francesca Cesati
and Team
Email: info@easywayitalia.com
Website: www.allencarr.com

JAPAN
Sessions held throughout Japan
www.allencarr.com

LATVIA
Tel: +371 67 27 22 25
Therapists: Anatolijs Ivanovs
Email: info@allencarr.lv
Website: www.allencarr.com

LEBANON
Opening 2013
Therapist: Sadeek El-Asaad
Website: www.allencarr.com

LITHUANIA
Tel: +370 694 29591
Therapist: Evaldas Zvirblis
Email: info@mestirukyti.eu
Website: www.allencarr.com

MAURITIUS
Tel: +230 5727 5103
Therapist: Heidi Hoareau
Email: info@allencarr.mu
Website: www.allencarr.com

MEXICO
Sessions held throughout Mexico
Tel: +52 55 2623 0631
Therapists: Jorge Davo and
Mario Campuzano Otero
Email: info@allencarr
-mexico.com
Website: www.allencarr.com

NETHERLANDS
*Sessions held throughout the
Netherlands*
Allen Carr's Easyway
'stoppen met roken'
Tel: (+31)53 478 43 62
(+31)900 786 77 37
Email: info@allencarr.nl
Website: www.allencarr.com

NEW ZEALAND
North Island – Auckland
Tel: +64 (0)9 817 5396
Therapist: Vickie Macrae
Email: vickie@easywaynz.co.nz
Website: www.allencarr.com

South Island - Christchurch
Tel: 0800 327992
Therapist: Laurence Cooke
Email: laurence
@easywaysouthisland.co.nz
Website: www.allencarr.com

NORWAY
Oslo
Tel: +47 93 20 09 11

Therapist: René Adde
Email: post@easyway-norge.no
Website: www.allencarr.com

PERU

Lima
Tel: +511 637 7310
Therapist: Luis Loranca
Email: lloranca
    @dejardefumaraltoque.com
Website: www.allencarr.com

POLAND

Sessions held throughout Poland
Tel: +48 (0)22 621 36 11
Therapist: Anna Kabat
Email: info@allen-carr.pl
Website: www.allencarr.com

PORTUGAL

Oporto
Tel: +351 22 9958698
Therapist: Ria Slof
Email: info@
    comodeixardefumar.com
Website: www.allencarr.com

ROMANIA

Tel: +40 (0) 7321 3 8383
Therapist: Diana Vasiliu
Email: raspunsuri@allencarr.ro
Website: www.allencarr.com

RUSSIA

Moscow
Tel: +7 495 644 64 26
Therapist: Alexander Formin
Email: info@allencarr.ru
Website: www.allencarr.com

ST. PETERSBURG

Opening 2013
Website: www.allencarr.com

SERBIA

Belgrade
Tel: +381 (0)11 308 8686
Email: office@allencarr.co.rs
    milos.rakovic@allencarr.co.rs
Website: www.allencarr.com

SINGAPORE

Tel: +65 6329 9660
Therapist: Pam Oei
Email: pam@allencarr.com.sg
Website: www.allencarr.com

SLOVENIA

Tel: 00386 (0) 40 77 61 77
Therapist: Gregor Server
Email: easyway@easyway.si
Website: www.allencarr.com

SOUTH AFRICA

Sessions held throughout South Africa

National Booking Line:
  0861 100 200
Head Office:
  15 Draper Square, Draper St,
  Claremont 7708, Cape Town
Cape Town: Dr Charles Nel
  Tel: +27 (0)21 851 5883
  Mobile: 083 600 5555
Therapists: Dr Charles Nel,
  Malcolm Robinson
  and Team
Email: easyway
  @allencarr.co.za
Website: www.allencarr.com

SOUTH KOREA
Opening 2013
Therapist: Yousung Cha
Website: www.allencarr.com

SPAIN

Madrid
Tel: +34 91 6296030
Therapist: Lola Camacho
Email: info@dejardefumar.org
Website: www.allencarr.com

Marbella
Tel: +44 8456 187306
Therapist:
  Charles Holdsworth Hunt
Email: stopsmoking
  @easywaymarbella.com
Sessions held in English
Website: www.allencarr.com

SWEDEN

Göteborge
Tel: +46 (0)8 240100
Email: info@allencarr.nu
Website: www.allencarr.com

Malmö
Tel: +46 (0) 40 30 24 00
Email: info@allencarr.nu
Website: www.allencarr.com

Stockholm
Tel: +46 (0) 735 000 123
Therapist: Christofer Elde
Email: kontakt@allencarr.se
Website: www.allencarr.com

SWITZERLAND
*Sessions held throughout
Switzerland*
Freephone: 0800RAUCHEN
  (0800/728 2436)
Tel: +41 (0)52 383 3773
Fax: +41 (0)52 3833774
Therapists: Cyrill Argast
  and Team
For sessions in Suisse Romand
and Svizzera Italiana:
  Tel: 0800 386 387
Email: info@allen-carr.ch
Website: www.allencarr.com

TURKEY
Sessions held throughout Turkey
Tel: +90 212 358 5307
Therapist: Emre Ustunucar

Email: info
@allencarrturkiye.com
Website: www.allencarr.com

UKRAINE

Crimea, Simferopol
Tel: +38 095 781 8180
Therapist: Yuriy Zhvakolyuk
Email
zhvakolyuk@gmail.com
Website: www.allencarr.com

Kiev
Tel: +38 044 353 2934
Therapist: Kirill Stekhin
Email: kirill@allencarr.kiev.ua
Website: www.allencarr.com

USA
Central information and
bookings:
Toll free: 1 866 666 4299
New York: 212- 330 9194
Email: info@theeasyway
tostopsmoking.com
Website: www.allencarr.com
Seminars held regularly in New
York, Los Angeles, Denver and
Houston. Corporate programs
available throughout the USA.
Mailing address:
1133 Broadway, Suite 706
New York, NY 10010
Therapists: Damian O'Hara,
Collene Curran, David Skeist

JOIN US!

Allen Carr's Easyway Clinics have spread throughout the world with incredible speed and success. Our global franchise network now covers more than 150 cities in over 45 countries. This amazing growth has been achieved entirely organically. Former addicts, just like you, were so impressed by the ease with which they stopped that they felt inspired to contact us to see how they could bring the method to their region.

If you feel the same, contact us for details on how to become an Allen Carr's Easyway To Stop Smoking or an Allen Carr's Easyway To Stop Drinking franchisee.

Email us at: join-us@allencarr.com including your full name, postal address and region of interest.

SUPPORT US!
No, don't send us money!

You have achieved something really marvellous. Every time we hear of someone escaping from the sinking ship, we get a feeling of enormous satisfaction.

It would give us great pleasure to hear that you have freed yourself from the slavery of addiction so please visit the following web page where you can tell us of your success, inspire others to follow in your footsteps and hear about ways you can help to spread the word.

www.allencarr.com/444/support-us

You can "like" our facebook page here
www.facebook.com/AllenCarr

Together, we can help further Allen Carr's mission: to cure the world of addiction.